CHRISTIAN COMFORT

CHRISTIAN COMFORT

Roger Ellsworth

EVANGELICAL PRESS

EVANGELICAL PRESS
Faverdale North Industrial Estate, Darlington,
DL3 0PH, England

Evangelical Press USA
P. O. Box 825, Webster, New York 14580, USA

e-mail: sales@evangelicalpress.org
web: http://www.evangelicalpress.org

First published 2003

**British Library Cataloguing in Publication Data
available**

ISBN 0 85234 540 2

Printed and bound in Great Britain by Creative Print
and Design Wales, Ebbw Vale, South Wales.

*The following chapters are dedicated to my dear
brothers in Christ,
Jim Dixon, Paul House and Bill Savage.*

ACKNOWLEDGEMENTS

I am thankful to the believers of Immanuel Baptist Church for the comfort and encouragement they have provided for me through our many years as pastor and people. I especially appreciate their interest in the preaching of God's Word. We have often been 'lost in wonder, love and praise' as we have looked at the comforting Scriptures covered in the chapters that follow.

I am also deeply indebted to my wife Sylvia, for constantly encouraging me in the ministry of writing and for making many helpful suggestions. As always, I must express profound thanks to my secretary, Laura Simmons, who has shared in the production of these chapters with her many impressive skills and with her trademark enthusiasm.

CONTENTS

INTRODUCTION

'Comfort' is one of the great words of the Bible. It means 'to alleviate grief by giving encouragement'.

My years in the pastorate have shown me that the people of God frequently need comfort. Christians often become despondent as they seek to cope with personal trials and afflictions and as they observe the abounding wickedness and the ever-increasing hostility of a godless world.

God is the source of the believer's comfort. He is, in the words of the apostle Paul, 'the God of all comfort' (2 Corinthians 1:3). The Apostle often seems to be an enigma, being at one and the same time a man of grief and a man of tremendous comfort. He certainly knew what it was to have grief, and in this letter to the Corinthians he lays before us the various forms of suffering he had to endure for the cause of Christ (11:24-33).

The church of Corinth was a major cause of the Apostle's grief. It was undoubtedly Paul's problem child. Riddled with dissension, filled with pride and arrogance, weak in doctrine and immature in understanding, careless about obedience — this was the church of Corinth.

In fact it had so many difficulties that Paul found it necessary to write four letters to it, two of which we do not possess. In the letter we know as 1 Corinthians, Paul dealt with the various problems of the church.

After sending that letter, Paul visited the church. However, his visit was marked by an ugly incident when, in a public meeting, one of the members insulted Paul, and the other members failed to come to his defence.

After that visit Paul sent Titus and another brother to Corinth with a further letter, which Paul characterizes as being written 'out of much affliction and anguish of heart with many tears'.

That letter, which we do not possess, achieved its intended purpose. After he had delivered it to Corinth, Titus was able to report to Paul that things had now been straightened out. Paul, greatly comforted, sent the letter that we know as 2 Corinthians, to convey his affection for the church, to clear up any remaining doubts about his apostleship and to pave the way for another visit.

As Paul reflected on what had transpired at Corinth, he realized that the positive turn of events there had occurred because of the hand of God. It was God who had alleviated his grief and encouraged his heart, and Paul now understood that God is the God of 'all comfort'.

Paul's delight in this God of all comfort can comfort us. Because we also know what it is to have sorrows that press us to breaking point, we need to explore Paul's description of God as the God of all comfort. So what can we draw from this?

All comfort comes from God

The first thing we must conclude is that all comfort comes from God. Do we understand the scope of what Paul is saying? If God is the God of all comfort, there is no comfort that arises apart from God. Anything that alleviates our sorrow and encourages our hearts comes to us from God. James puts the same truth in these words: 'Every good gift and every perfect gift is from above, and comes down from the Father of lights, with whom there is no variation or shadow of turning' (James 1:17).

Do you find comfort in your family? God instituted the family and gave you your family. Do you find comfort in your church? The church was God's idea. Do you find comfort in the beauties of creation? God is the Creator of all things. Do you find comfort in pleasure? God is the one who gave us all the things that bring pleasure to us, and when they are used in accordance with his will, they give pleasure. Do you find your comfort in work? God is the one who gave you the ability to do your work, and he is the one who made work satisfying.

Perhaps someone will say, 'If all comfort comes from God, how are we to explain that so many find comfort in sin?' The answer to that is very simple. There is no comfort in sin. Flying in the face of the commands of God may seem to alleviate our sorrows and bring peace to our hearts for a while but, when all is said and done, we will be made keenly aware that there is no comfort in sin. It always makes great promises, but it never delivers. It offers peace but brings sorrow. It offers comfort but only brings heartache and ruin. The Lord says:

> But the wicked are like the troubled sea,
> When it cannot rest,
> Whose waters cast up mire and dirt.
> 'There is no peace,'
> Says my God, 'for the wicked'
>
> (Isaiah 57:20-21).

God has comfort for every sorrow

A second truth we may glean from Paul's description of God as the God of all comfort may be stated in this way: there is no sorrow or grief for which God does not have comfort.

What is your grief or sorrow today? Do you dread the thought of leaving this life and standing before God? Are you acutely aware that you are a guilty sinner and that he is a perfectly holy God? Are you keenly aware that you deserve nothing but his judgement?

God has comfort for you! He tells you that he has made a way for guilty sinners to stand clean and guiltless before him on the Day of Judgement. That way is his Son, Jesus Christ. The Lord Jesus Christ, by his perfect life and by his death on the cross, has done everything necessary for sinners to be forgiven of their sins.

Has a friend turned against you? God has comfort for you. He tells you that he is a friend who sticks closer than a brother (Proverbs 18:24) and that, although all others forsake you, he will not (Hebrews 13:5-6).

Do you have a child that is living in rebellion against the Lord? God has comfort for you! He says that if that child has been trained in the right way 'when he is old he will not depart from it' (Proverbs 22:6).

Are you uncertain about what the future holds for you? God has comfort for you! He says,

> Trust in the LORD with all your heart,
> And lean not on your own understanding;
> In all your ways acknowledge him,
> And he shall direct your paths
>
> (Proverbs 3:5-6).

Have you lost a loved one? Do you feel that you yourself may have to face death very soon? God has comfort for you! He assures you in his Word that this life is not all there is, that for the child of God this life is not even the best there is. Scripture tells us that death for Christians means their souls go immediately into the presence of their loving heavenly Father.

Death is not even the end for their bodies. One glorious day the Lord Jesus himself will return. The archangel will shout, heaven's trumpet will sound and the bodies of all those who died in the faith will be raised from their graves and reunited to their souls. Christians who are still living at that time will be caught up to meet the Lord in the air, and there the greatest of all reunions will take place.

Oh, how comforting this is! It is no wonder the Apostle concluded his description of it with these words: 'Therefore comfort one another with these words' (1 Thessalonians 4:13-18).

But what about that person who has lost a loved one who did not know the Lord Jesus Christ as his Lord and Saviour? Surely there can be no comfort for that! But there is. The book of Revelation says, 'And God will wipe away every tear from their eyes; there shall be no more death, nor sorrow, nor crying. There shall be no more pain, for the former things have passed away' (Revelation 21:4). While the child of God sorrows here for his loved ones who die without Christ, he knows there is coming a day when he will sorrow no more.

Nothing is more satisfying and thrilling to the child of God than scouring the Word of God to find comfort and consolation for the various burdens and trials of life.

The comforted are to comfort

But we must not stop there. Paul's words to the Corinthians reveal that God does not want us merely to hoard comfort for ourselves. As we find comfort in the God of all comfort, we are, in turn, to comfort others. Paul says God gives us comfort 'that we may be able to comfort those who are in any trouble, with the comfort with which we ourselves are comforted by God' (2 Corinthians 1:4). Christians are not, therefore, reservoirs merely to hold comfort, but rivers to channel comfort to others.

I have affirmed that God has comfort for all the trials and tribulations life brings our way. And yet we all know that there are many who are living without comfort. The trials of life have them in a constant state of anxiety and agitation. It is not that God has not made comfort available. He has. It is rather that the comfort he has made available is not reaching them. And why is this so? Could it be that those of us who have found comfort in our own trials are not channelling that comfort? Here is a brother in Christ who is going through great trials, a brother whom we could help with the comfort we ourselves have received. But we are too busy. So our dear brother continues to struggle along. Here is an unsaved friend who needs the comfort of the gospel, and we know all about this comfort, but we, out of fear of offending him or out of sheer indifference, have not shared it.

Let us search ourselves on this matter of comfort. Let us give thanks to our God for being the God of all comfort. Let us go to his Word to find comfort when trials arise. And let us make sure we are constantly on the watch for that person who needs the very comfort that we ourselves have found in the Lord.

HOW TO USE *THE GUIDE*

Christian comfort is the sixth book in a new series called *The Guide*. This series will cover books of the Bible on an individual basis, such as *Ecclesiastes*, and relevant topics such as this one on comfort. The series aim is to communicate the Christian faith in a straightforward and readable way.

Each book in *The Guide* will cover a book of the Bible or topic in some detail, but will be contained in relatively short and concise chapters. There will be questions at the end of each chapter for personal study or group discussion, to help you to study the Word of God more deeply.

An innovative and exciting feature of *The Guide* is that it is linked to its own web site. As well as being encouraged to search God's Word for yourself, you are invited to ask questions related to the book on the web site, where you will not only be able to have your own questions answered, but also be able to see a selection of answers that have been given to other readers. The web site can be found at www.evangelicalpress.org/ TheGuide. Once you are on the site you just need to click on the 'select' button at the top of the page, according to the book on which you wish to post a question. Your question will then be answered by either

Michael Bentley, the web site co-ordinator and author of *Colossians and Philemon*, or others who have been selected because of their experience, their understanding of the Word of God and their dedication to working for the glory of the Lord.

Other books that have already been published include *Ecclesiastes*, *The Bible book by book*, *Esther* and *Revolutionary forgiveness*, which is the first in the topical series. Many more will follow. It is the publisher's hope that you will be stirred to think more deeply about the Christian faith, and will be helped and encouraged in living out your Christian life, through the study of God's Word, in the difficult and demanding days in which we live.

CHAPTER ONE

COMFORT FOR THOSE WHO ARE TROUBLED BY GOD'S WAYS

LOOK IT UP

BIBLE REFERENCE

Indeed these are the mere edges of his ways,
And how small a whisper we hear of him!
But the thunder of his power who can understand?
(Job 26:14).

Suggested further reading: Isaiah 40:12-31

INTRODUCTION

A truth capsule

I stand and look at the starry sky, and I say, 'What a great God created this!', and Job calls to me from the pages of Scripture and says, 'You are just seeing the edge.' I stand before the mountains and I am amazed at their majesty and enormity, and I say, 'What a great God created these mountains!' And Job calls to me and says, 'You are just seeing the edge.' I go to the ocean and hear the waves crashing on the shore and I say, 'What a great God created this!' And Job calls to me: 'You are only hearing a whisper!' I hear the thunder, and I say, 'What kind of God is it that can make it thunder like that!' And Job says, 'This is a mere whisper!'

How great God must be if what we are seeing is just the edge! How great God must be if we are just hearing a mere whisper!

Some points to ponder

A breathtaking tour

The story of Job is well known. Although he was a right-eous man, Job had to endure indescribable suffering. After losing all his children and all his possessions, he was afflicted with grievous boils.

Eliphaz, Bildad and Zophar came to provide comfort for Job, but he was not impressed with their efforts. He called them 'miserable comforters' (16:2) and charged them with speaking 'words of wind' (16:3). He essentially said, 'You fellows aren't very good at this at all.'

Most of the book of Job is taken up with dialogue between Job and these men. As we read these exchanges, we come to understand that Job is a study in true faith. There were times in his immense suffering when he appeared to be on the verge of losing his faith. But true faith always rallies. That is its nature. It can never be extinguished. It can flicker, but it can never be quenched.

We have one of faith's rallies in this twenty-sixth chapter. Here Job responds to the stuffy, intellectual Bildad. Job reminds him of the greatness of God. He does so by taking him on a tour that begins in the dark recesses of the grave and hell (vv. 5-6) and ascends to the very throne of God and the pillars of heaven (v. 11). He then drops to the sea (v. 12) before ascending to the starry skies (v. 13).

In the course of giving Bildad this tour, Job makes some astounding assertions. He affirms that God has suspended the earth on nothing (v. 7), that he fills the clouds with water (v. 8), and that he stirs up the sea and controls all the storms (v. 12). Job further asserts that God adorns the heavens with the stars (v. 13).

THINK ABOUT IT

THINK ABOUT IT

The Milky Way galaxy is so massive that travelling at the speed of light, we would be able to cross only one-tenth of it in six thousand years. Astronomers say there are billions of such galaxies. The prophet Isaiah tells us that God measures the heavens as the distance between the tip of the thumb and the tip of the little finger! (Isaiah 40:12).

The Atlantic Ocean covers 41 million square miles and contains 85 million cubic miles of water. The Pacific Ocean covers 69 million square miles and contains 141 million cubic miles of water. All the oceans of the world contain 329 cubic miles of water and have an average depth of 12,400 feet. Here is the greatness of God: the prophet Isaiah says he holds the waters of the earth in the palm of his hand (40:12).

It is a breathtaking tour. But even more breathtaking is the assertion with which Job ends it. Having affirmed all these marvellous and awe-inspiring things about God and his works, Job says they constitute nothing more than the edges of his ways and a small whisper.

What an amazing statement! Job has summoned, as it were, all the powers of his imagination and all his eloquence to take Bildad on this tour of the greatness of God and, after it is finished, he says they had only seen the edges of God. They had heard only a mere whisper.

Do we understand what Job was saying? The edge of something represents only a very small portion of the whole reality. A whisper represents only a little of the total volume. The edge leaves much to be seen and the whisper much to be heard. With all the evidences for the glory, power, majesty, splendour and wisdom of God we see in the created order, we are seeing just a tiny fraction of all that there is to see.

We are face to face, then, with the reality that no matter how much we know about the greatness and glory of God, we know very little indeed. The apostle Paul said as much in these words, 'Oh, the depth of the riches both of the wisdom and knowledge of God! How unsearchable are his judgements and his ways past finding out!' (Romans 11:33).

If we could only come to a better understanding of the greatness of God, we would be better ourselves! We would be better in worship. We would be better

in prayer. We would be better in Bible study; and we would be better in obeying God's commandments.

What shall we do, then, in the light of the fact that we know and understand very little about our glorious God?

Thank God for the edges

We are not seeing much of God but, thanks to God himself, we are seeing something. If I were to hold an object before you and hide all of it from your view except the edge, would that edge be real? Of course it would. And you would say, 'I can only see the edge, but that edge is real. It represents something larger.'

You would not look at that edge and say, 'That edge indicates that nothing is there.' No, you would say just the opposite, that the edge indicates something far greater that is hidden from view.

Just because we see only a small portion of God and his ways does not mean that God is not there. It means he *is* there. Some seem to say, 'We know so little about God, he must not be there at all.' What incredible logic that is! Just the opposite is true. The edges indicate the reality.

While the edges of God's ways are on display in a general way in the created order, they are displayed even more fully in the Lord Jesus

Christ. How thankful we should be for him! He, the second person of the Trinity, took upon himself our humanity, and in doing so revealed more of God. The apostle John puts it in these words: 'And the Word became flesh and dwelt among us, and we beheld his glory, the glory as of the only begotten of the Father, full of grace and truth' (John 1:14).

THINK ABOUT IT

An unbeliever wrote these lines in the *American Magazine*: 'The agnostic may face life with a smile and a heroic attitude. He may put on a brave front, but he is not happy. He stands in awe and reverence before the vastness and majesty of the universe, knowing not whence he came nor why. He is appalled at the stupendousness of space and the infinitude of time, humiliated by the infinite smallness of himself, cognizant of his own frailty, weakness, and brevity. Certainly he sometimes yearns for a staff on which to lean. He, too, carries a cross. For him, this earth is but a tricky raft adrift in the unfathomable waters of eternity with no horizon in sight. His heart aches for every precious life upon the raft — drifting, drifting, drifting, wither no one knows.'[1]

The fact that we now see only the edges of God's ways should have special meaning for us when we

come up against difficulties and hardships as
Job did. The truth he uttered regarding the edges
of God's ways had to mean much to him. He
was in the crucible of unspeakably severe suffering. What a comfort it was for him to be able
to say, 'My sufferings are the edges of God's ways.
I do not understand all that he is doing, but I
know there is more to this than I can see.'

Every child of God can say the same about
his sufferings. They are just the edges of God's
ways. He has far greater purposes in our difficulties than we will ever realize in this life.

If you are suffering today, try to understand
that you are not seeing the whole picture. All
you are seeing is just an edge. And try to understand that there is a great purpose in what you
are going through and that purpose will eventually be clear.

REMEMBER THIS

A day is coming when God's people will
not have to look at the edges any longer.
They will see the whole reality. The apostle
Paul says, 'For now we see in a mirror, dimly,
but then face to face. Now I know in part,
but then I shall know just as I also am known'
(1 Corinthians 13:12). And when God shows
us the whole picture, we shall surely acknowledge that he has done all things well.

What a day it will be when God's people are finally taken from this world of sorrow and difficulty into the presence of God and all the dark things are made plain! Even in our best moments we have never understood what heaven is all about. In the twenty-first chapter of Revelation, John takes us farther than anyone else. He says there is no crying there, no sorrow, tears are wiped away, and there is no more death.

QUESTIONS FOR DISCUSSION

1. What effect should the greatness of God have upon our worship? Read Psalms 95 and 96.

2. What does the greatness of God tell us about our priorities? Read Jeremiah 9:23-24.

3. The Lord Jesus Christ claimed to reveal God the Father (John 14:9). What are some of the major evidences that Jesus was God in human flesh? Read John 5:31-47; 10:31-39; 14:10-11; Acts 2:22-36; 13:29-41; Romans 1:4.

THE GUIDE

CHAPTER TWO

COMFORT FOR THE ANXIOUS AND FEARFUL

LOOK IT UP

BIBLE REFERENCE

You number my wanderings;
Put my tears into your bottle;
Are they not in your book?
(Psalm 56:8).

Suggested reading: Psalm 91:1-16

INTRODUCTION

A truth capsule

The word 'wanderings' comes from a Hebrew word, which can also be translated 'flutterings'. We associate the word 'flutter' with an absence of peace. It means to be in a state of excitement or turmoil. A fluttering bird is not at peace. It is agitated and frightened.

Life in this world has a way of making us feel like fluttering birds. We like to think of ourselves as being strong, poised and in control, but then some circumstance arises that makes that same strength, poise and control go right out of the window, and we find ourselves fluttering. There is no end to such unsettling problems in our world.

Some points to ponder

Fluttering David? It almost sounds like a square circle. This is the same David who stood with calm composure in front of the giant Goliath before bouncing a stone off his head and dropping him dead to the ground.

It would seem that nothing could ruffle David; but something did. Shortly after his victory over Goliath, David found that he was the object of the fierce hatred of his own king. So intense was Saul's loathing that David was forced to flee. He did not stop running until he came to Gath in the land of the Philistines. There he soon realized that he had not solved his problems but only compounded them. He was surrounded by many who wanted nothing less than to carry his head around on a stake. There he cried:

> Be merciful to me, O God, for man would swallow
>   me up;
> Fighting all day he oppresses me.
> My enemies would hound me all day,
> For there are many who fight against me, O Most
>   High.
>
> ...
>
> All day they twist my words;
> All their thoughts are against me for evil.
> They gather together,
> They hide, they mark my steps,
> When they lie in wait for my life
>
> (Psalm 56:1-2, 5-6).

THINK ABOUT IT

David's phrase 'they twist my words' means that his enemies had distorted and misrepresented his words. This reminds us of how very careful we must be when we speak. Knowing their accountability to God for their speaking and how much harm evil irresponsible words can do, God's people seek to speak with grace, having, as it were, their speech 'seasoned with salt' (Colossians 4:6). Salt, as a preservative, retards corruption and rottenness. Christians strive to avoid all corrupt speech.

The unflutterable David was now fluttering! But he tells us here how he was able to overcome his flutterings and find peace and rest. His relief came from realizing God has a calculator for numbering his flutterings, a bottle for catching his tears, and a book for explaining the flutterings of the saints (Psalm 56:8).

God's calculator

The New King James Version puts the word 'number' in the present tense, and therefore has David affirming that God was counting his flutterings as he, David, experienced them. But other versions put the word 'number' in the past tense and, therefore, have David affirming that God had already numbered them in advance.

We will leave the language experts to wrangle over that. While they are doing so, we can find help by dwelling on that past tense. There is tremendous consolation in knowing that there is a limit to our flutterings. God has already given them an exact number, and we will not have one more than he has designed. And one day we will have no more at all.

God's bottle

That brings us to consider God's bottle. David asks the Lord to put his tears into his bottle. It sounds like a very strange request, but when we stop to consider it we find it has rich implications. For one thing, for God to catch David's tears in a bottle, he would have to be aware that David was crying. In other words, he would have to see David's tears. The Bible assures us that God watches closely over all human events, that nothing escapes his all-seeing eye. That eye is especially on his children (2 Chronicles 16:9; Job 31:4; Psalm 34:15).

Now, dear child of God, there are times when your heart is broken, and you think for all the world that no one knows or cares. Let this precious truth console and comfort you. You have never shed a single tear of heartache that your Father in heaven has not taken note of.

Not one has ever rolled down your cheek and dropped to the ground, that your Father did not see; and not one ever will.

Then there is another thing. For God to catch David's tears in a bottle, he, God, would have to be very near indeed. It would not be possible to catch someone's tears in a bottle unless you are right in front of the person who is weeping.

The Word of God also assures us that God is ever near his people. He never leaves nor forsakes them (Hebrews 13:5). When they weep with sorrow, he is near. But the primary thing David had in mind when he asked God to put his tears in a bottle was the idea of preservation. He wanted God to preserve his tears.

People preserve lots of things. A young lady will take a flower from a corsage she wore on a special occasion and press it between the pages of a scrapbook. Parents preserve the childhood years of their youngsters by taking countless pictures and running miles of film through their video cameras.

In like manner, God preserves the tears of his people. They will never be lost. While God will wipe all the tears from the eyes of his people on the dawning of that great eternal day, he himself will never forget a single tear that they shed. And it will be his joy and delight in eternity to pour out comfort and blessing in place of those sorrows.

THINK ABOUT IT

The author of Psalm 91 depicts a wide range of problems that can make us anxious:

- 'the snare of the fowler' (v. 3) — difficulties that come unexpectedly upon us
- 'perilous pestilence' (v. 3) — anxieties we pick up from those around us
- the 'terror by night' (v. 5) — those distressing thoughts that fly through our minds when we try to sleep
- 'the arrow that flies by day' (v. 5) — anxieties that come to us because of the hostility of others. Arrows do not just fly, they have to be shot!
- 'the pestilence that walks in darkness' (v. 6) — those dangers that strike when we think we are most safe, that is, at night when we have gone home
- 'the destruction that lays waste at noonday' (v. 6) — calamities that arise when we are in our most productive years
- 'stones' (v. 12) — damage we bring upon ourselves by being preoccupied and undiscerning. Stones do not strike or pounce, but they inflict real pain on the careless traveller who stubs his toe.

With all these causes for anxiety, the psalmist found peace by making the Lord his refuge (v. 9).

God's book

Finally, David makes mention of God's book
(v. 8). He affirms that his flutterings are already
in God's book. We surely understand this. One
of the primary purposes of a book is to explain
something to the readers. It is to give them insight into something that they have not yet
understood.

We certainly do not understand all the trials
and tears of this life, but God has already written
them down in his book, where they are all ex-
plained. We may rest assured that when we get
to heaven, God will pull that book from his shelf
and read to us from it. He will turn to that chapter which chronicles your life and you will then
understand the reason for all your flutterings,
trials and tears. He will turn to that chapter in
which my life is recorded, and I will at last understand the reason for all my flutterings.

Charles Tindley expresses this truth very well
in these familiar lines:

Trials dark on every hand,
And we cannot understand
All the ways that God would lead us
To that blessed promised land;
But He'll guide us with His eye,
And we'll follow till we die,
And we will understand it better by and by.

EXPLANATION

Oft our cherished plans have failed,
Disappointments have prevailed,
And we've wandered in the darkness,
Heavy-hearted and alone;
But we're trusting in the Lord,
And according to His word,
We will understand it better by and by.[1]

REMEMBER THIS

Many seem to think that God will have to apologize to them on that day. They picture themselves marching up to him and saying, 'You let this and that happen to me, and my life was ruined.' And they imagine God saying, 'Oh dear, I didn't realize all that. I guess I really made a mistake. I'm sorry.'

But God will not have to apologize to anyone. He did not put us on this earth for our comfort but for his glory, and on that day when he reads from his book every child of God will finally understand how the flutterings of life promoted the glory of God.

I'll bless the hand that guided,
I'll bless the heart that planned,
When throned where glory dwelleth
In Immanuel's land.[2]

Our problem is that we want God to read that book of explanation now. We want him to explain our flutterings

to us while we are still in this life. But God does not read that book to us now. Instead he gives us a book to read, the Bible, and that book tells us to keep trusting him and serving him until that unspeakably great day when he reads to us from his Book of Life.

QUESTIONS FOR DISCUSSION

DISCUSS IT

1. Read Revelation 5:8. What does the Lord preserve in addition to the tears of his people? What does this tell us about the importance God attaches to this particular keepsake? How important is it to you?

2. Read Matthew 6:26-34; Philippians 4:6-7; 1 Peter 5:7. What do these Scriptures teach about driving anxious care from our lives?

3. Gath was a strange place for David to go. Can you think of some more saints of God in strange places? Read Genesis 12:10-20; 13:1-13.

THE GUIDE

CHAPTER THREE

COMFORT FOR THE SUFFERING

BIBLE REFERENCE

'My brethren, count it all joy when you fall into various trials, knowing that the testing of your faith produces patience. But let patience have its perfect work, that you may be perfect and complete, lacking nothing' (James 1:2-4).

Suggested reading: 2 Corinthians 4:7-14

A truth capsule

James' phrase 'when you fall into various trials...' (v. 2) reveals the certainty of trials. It was not a matter of *whether* they were going to come, but only *when*. The apostle Paul also affirms this truth (Philippians 1:29; 1 Thessalonians 3:3). The question in the mind of the Christian is not whether trials will come but rather how to deal with them when they arrive.

Some points to ponder

It was not the purpose of James to give us a full-blown theology of suffering. He makes only a brief mention of it before moving on. But by ranging over the Scriptures we can in general find certain guidelines and principles for helping us to cope with the trials that come our way.

Suffering we bring on ourselves

First of all, Scripture would have us to distinguish between suffering we bring upon ourselves and suffering the Lord brings on us.

In addressing the matter of persecution, the apostle Peter made this distinction. He told his readers to make sure the persecution that came their way was undeserved (1 Peter 4:15-16).

The law of sowing and reaping is still in effect. Our choices lead to consequences. If we make good choices we can expect good consequences, but if we make evil choices we can expect evil consequences.

If we abuse our bodies, our health will deteriorate, and we may very well go to an early grave. If we abuse those around us, our relationships are going to deteriorate. If we fail to feed and nurture ourselves spiritually, our walk with God is going to suffer.

We all know these things are true, but when the consequences of evil choices begin to pour in, we are ever inclined to ignore the law of sowing and reaping and lament our circumstances by crying out: 'Why is God doing this to me?'

In this situation God is only letting us experience the consequences of what we ourselves have chosen. The proper response to this type of suffering is to break the pattern of behaviour that has brought the suffering upon us.

THINK ABOUT IT

Otto Von Bismarck, chancellor of Germany during World War I, allowed himself to be consumed with hate. One morning he announced proudly: 'I have spent the whole night hating.'

Bismarck paid a fearful price for the kind of life he chose. He grew a beard to hide the twitching muscles of his face. Jaundice, gastric ulcers, gallstones and shingles plagued him. He died at eighty-three, 'an embittered, cynical, desperately lonely old man, miserable and self-consumed'.[1]

Suffering from God's hand

But let us now turn to the form of suffering that most troubles Christians: the suffering that comes, as far as we can tell, apart from the evil choices we make. How do we handle this type of suffering?

The crucial thing is to remember that such suffering comes from God's hand. Nothing is clearer in Scripture than the truth that God sends trials and difficulties into the lives of his children in order to achieve certain purposes.

Consider the suffering of Joseph, for example. It came upon him in wave after wave. His hateful brothers sold him into slavery. He ended up in Egypt where he was framed for something he did not do and was cast into prison.

It all came upon him through no real fault of his own. Joseph must have spent a large amount of his time wondering why all these things had happened to him. Years later he had his answer, and was able to see that God had a purpose in it all. It was so that he, Joseph, could be the means of saving his people from terrible famine. Joseph put it in these words: 'But as for you, you meant evil against me; but God meant it for good, in order to bring it about as it is this day, to save many people alive' (Genesis 50:20).

THINK ABOUT IT

When God wants to drill a man
And thrill a man
And skill a man,
When God wants to mould a man
To play the noblest part;
When He yearns with all His heart
To create so great and bold a man
That all the world shall be amazed,
Watch His methods, watch His ways!
How He ruthlessly perfects
Whom He royally elects!
How He hammers him and hurts him,
And with mighty blows converts him

Into trial shapes of clay which
Only God understands;
While his tortured heart is crying
And he lifts beseeching hands!
How He bends but never breaks
When his good He undertakes;
How He uses whom He chooses
And with every purpose fuses him;
By every act induces him
To try His splendour out —
God knows what He's about![2]

(Oswald Chambers)

Other Scriptures also give testimony to God's purposes in sending suffering. The psalmist writes:

EXPLANATION

Before I was afflicted I went astray,
But now I keep your word
...
It is good for me that I have been afflicted,
That I may learn your statutes

(Psalm 119:67, 71).

A few verses later he adds:

I know, O LORD, that your judgements are right,
And that in faithfulness you have afflicted
me

(v. 75).

Yes, God sometimes sends suffering to chastise us for our sins and make us more scrupulous about obeying his commands (Hebrews 12:5-11).

Sometimes God's purpose in sending suffering is to make our faith strong and to make us more Christlike. One aspect of Christlikeness is patience, a virtue James specifically says is produced by trials.

Sometimes God sends suffering in order that his people may demonstrate their faith in him. We may rest assured that unbelievers are always watching how we react to the difficulties of life. They formulate their views of Christianity from what they see or do not see in us. If they see us continuing to trust and serve the Lord in the midst of our suffering, they will be convinced that there is something to our faith. If they see us respond to our suffering by becoming hard and bitter towards God, they will feel justified in concluding that there is nothing to our faith.

God's purpose in sending suffering is always to bring glory to himself. The apostle Peter says faith that is 'tested by fire' will at last be found to bring 'praise, honour and glory' to Christ. In this life, we are not always able to see how our suffering can possibly bring honour to God. But it is not necessary for us to see it in order for it to be true.

How does God derive glory from our suffering? Over here is a Christian who has suffered terrible illness for a long time, and he says he would not have been able to bear it if God had not been with him to strengthen and help him. That brings glory to God.

Over there is a Christian who has suffered financial hardship, and he talks about how the promises of God have encouraged and comforted him through it all. When God's faithfulness to his promises is emphasized, God is glorified.

REMEMBER THIS

We can find strength to face suffering by looking to that unspeakably glorious time when all our sufferings will finally be over.

Yes, such a time is coming! The Bible assures us that it is true. The tears of this life will be wiped away. Sorrow will dissolve. Death itself will be crushed finally and for ever. The Bible constantly warns us not to become so intoxicated with this life that we fail to look beyond it to the life to come.

That forward look has the marvellous ability to transform the suffering of this present time. As we dwell on the glory to be revealed we shall most certainly find ourselves saying with the apostle Paul, 'For I consider that the sufferings of this present time are not worthy to be compared with the glory which shall be revealed in us' (Romans 8:18).

And let us never forget how it is that we have confidence regarding life to come. It is through no merit of our own, but solely because of the redeeming work of our Lord Jesus Christ on Calvary's cross.

QUESTIONS FOR DISCUSSION

1. What are some of the things God has promised to his people regarding their difficulties and trials? Read Romans 8:28; 2 Corinthians 4:16-18.

2. Selwyn Hughes says of the Christian's suffering: 'The darkening clouds may only serve to quicken your pace towards Home.'[3] What will the Christian's eternal home be like? Read Revelation 21 & 22.

3. Read 2 Corinthians 11:22-33. How many separate instances of suffering can you identify in the apostle Paul's ministry?

CHAPTER FOUR

COMFORT FOR THE BROKEN-HEARTED

BIBLE REFERENCE

'And she was in bitterness of soul, and prayed to the
LORD and wept in anguish'
(1 Samuel 1:10).

Suggested reading: Psalm 31

A truth capsule

The Bible tells us that God is sovereign, that not
a sparrow falls that he does not know about, not
a single hair on our heads goes unnoticed or
uncounted. However we choose to explain our
suffering in this life, one thing we cannot say is
that it takes place without God's knowledge or
permission. This truth troubles some deeply, but
it is a great comfort to me to know that nothing
can come my way that my loving heavenly Father
does not allow.

Some points to ponder

Elkanah had two wives, Hannah and Peninnah,
and there was much turmoil in his home. This
should not come as a surprise to us. The Lord
made it clear from the very beginning of human

history that marriage should be monogamous, but Elkanah had ignored this command. Polygamy was the accepted practice of his day and Elkanah went along with it. The mistake he made is one God's people are still making. How we need to learn that just because something has become accepted in our society does not mean it is right!

The turmoil in Elkanah's home centred around the ability of his wives to bear children. Peninnah had children, but Hannah did not. One would think a woman with children would certainly sympathize with a childless woman, but not Peninnah. She never missed a chance to ridicule Hannah and make her feel a failure.

THINK ABOUT IT

In this age in which abortion and infanticide have become so very common, it is essential for God's people to understand that children are a gift from the Lord (Genesis 48:8-9). They are also his heritage and his reward (Psalm 127:3). We need to remember that children are a sacred trust and it is our responsibility to 'bring them up in the training and admonition of the Lord' (Ephesians 6:4).

It is not hard to figure out which was the better of these two women. Peninnah was obviously cruel, unfeeling and wicked, but from what we read in the first two chapters of 1 Samuel, Hannah was a godly, sensitive, loving woman.

EXPLANATION

Here we have, then, a wicked woman who had been blessed with children, and a godly woman who had not. We are peering into a dark dilemma. Why should a godly person suffer such disappointment and heartbreak? The other question surrounding this dilemma concerns why wicked people should be more blessed than those who are godly. It is not that we do not want people without God to be blessed; it is more a matter of why they often seem to be more blessed than the righteous. Shouldn't serving God count for something?

Why? We often ask that question, but we seldom have it answered to our satisfaction. Hannah's experience certainly does not give us the answers to all our questions, but it does give us something of real value. It tells us how to live with our 'whys' until they finally disintegrate in the glory of God's presence.

Do not leave God out

First, we learn from Hannah's experience that we are not to leave out God when we explain our disappointments. This is what many do. When a disappointment or a difficulty arises, they explain it by saying God had nothing to do with it.

All parents know the helpless feeling of not being able to keep our children from harm and danger. We try, but there is always that unforeseen something that happens suddenly to injure our children.

Many people see God in the same way. As far as they are concerned, God is the great concerned parent in the sky. He tries very hard to keep his children out of harm's way, but there is always something that pops up and takes him by surprise. When these people finally confront God with why they had to face some great trial, they fully expect him to shrug his shoulders, shake his head in dismay, and say, 'We tried to prevent it but couldn't. Hope you understand.'

The image of a well-meaning deity who bumbles and fumbles his way along has become etched indelibly in the minds of many through the books and films of the last several years. We envision a God who struggles along with incompetent staff, computer foul-ups and unforeseen circumstances.

But a well-meaning, helpless God is not the explanation for Hannah's disappointment. Scripture flatly says she was not able to bear children because 'the Lord had closed her womb' (1 Samuel 1:5-6).

We can wonder all we want about why God would do such a thing, but the Bible closes the option of saying God had nothing to do with it.

Do not feel hard towards God

The second thing Hannah's experience of disappointment teaches us is that we are not to harden our hearts towards God when we encounter disappointing experiences.

Most Christians do not make the first mistake we have looked at. They know God is not a help-less parent who wrings his hands in despair over the trials of his children. But they have not quite been able to suppress their feelings of bitterness towards God. They seem to take the view that they can get even with God: 'If God allowed this to happen to me, I'll get even with him by not going to church.' From all indications, there are a lot of bitter Christians today. They believe God has not dealt with them fairly, that they deserve far better than they have received.

All who feel such bitterness lose sight of one great fact — God sends trials and disappoint-ments our way because he has far nobler purposes in mind than we can possibly compre-hend, purposes that always have the best interests of his children at heart.

Hannah could have felt bitterness and hard-ness towards God about her disappointment, but she did not. She had 'bitterness of soul' (v. 10), but that only means her childlessness was pain-ful for her. It does not mean she was angry at God about it. If she had been bitter towards God she would never have referred to herself three times as the Lord's 'maidservant' (v. 11). What is a 'maidservant'? It is a woman who exists solely for the purpose of carrying out the desires of her master, and Hannah saw the Lord as her Master.

What mattered most to Hannah, therefore, was not what she wanted but what her God wanted. And what God wanted was far greater than Hannah ever imagined. God wanted a Samuel to lead a sinful nation back to himself. It was through closing Hannah's womb for a period of several years that God got his Samuel.

What was necessary for this to happen? If Samuel had come quickly and easily to Hannah she would not have been inclined to feel any extra measure of gratitude, and if she had not felt any extra gratitude she would not have devoted Samuel to the Lord from his childhood.

As a result of enduring the trial without bitterness, then, Hannah discovered that God indeed had a far greater purpose in mind — the good of the whole nation. And she also discovered that he had her own interests at heart. Hannah was rewarded for enduring the trial God sent to her. She was undoubtedly brought to a higher level of commitment and trust than she ever occupied before. And she ended up having three more sons and two daughters (2:21).

It is often hard for us to accept, but our God does all things well. He does indeed work 'all things ... together for good' for his children (Romans 8:28).

Do not give up on God

The third thing Hannah teaches us is that we should not give up on God for not easing our disappointments. Hannah did not know why God had allowed the disappointment of not bearing a child to come to her, but there were some things she did know. She knew that although she had this trial it did not necessarily mean it was permanent. She knew God had the power to lift the trial from her. And she knew that prayer is the channel God uses to employ his power on behalf of his people.

So she began to pray. How she prayed! She did not mechanically mouth a few set clichés, but poured her heart out to the Lord. She told him of the depth of her anguish. She told him the great desire of her heart for a son. But, as we have seen, she recognized the Lord's sovereign right to do as he pleases and gladly took her place as his servant.

Good always comes from such praying, and so it was with Hannah. The most obvious good she received is stated in the words: 'it came to pass in the process of time that Hannah conceived and bore a son' (v. 20).

Eugene Peterson writes: 'All suffering, all pain, all emptiness, all disappointment is seed: sow it in God, and He will, finally, bring a crop of joy from it.'[1] But the fact is that Hannah received good before she ever conceived. Verse 18 tells us that after she prayed 'her face was no longer sad'. Even before the trial was removed she received peace regarding it.

What trial do you carry today? What disappointment troubles and vexes you? Does it seem as if God has forgotten you in the midst of your troubles? Take comfort from this — the trial can be eased through believing prayer.

God may not deal with us as he did with Hannah, but we certainly must deal with him as Hannah did. He may not see fit to remove the trial from us, any more than he saw fit to remove a trial that greatly troubled the apostle Paul. But if God decides to leave the trial, we can rest assured he will remove the crushing sadness of the trial by giving us the grace to bear it (2 Corinthians 12:7-10).

When trials come, then, we must go to God in prayer, tell him how deeply the trial hurts, and ask him to either remove it or give us grace to bear it without bitterness. And we must ask him to help us trust him while we endure the trial; trust that he has a wise purpose in his mind and our best interests in his heart.

THINK ABOUT IT

The second chapter of 1 Samuel records another prayer offered by Hannah. This prayer, which occupies only ten verses, mentions God twenty-three times. We can say, therefore, that while Hannah glanced at her circumstances, she gazed at her God. How very often we gaze at our problems and glance at God!

If we will learn from Hannah and gaze at God, we shall find the resources we need for facing the challenges of life.

DISCUSS IT

If we are to do well in child-rearing we must remember that great men and women usually have great parents, and great parents have a great God.

QUESTIONS FOR DISCUSSION

1. Read Psalm 73. How did its author Asaph find peace about the age-old problem of the prosperity of the wicked?

2. What is the future of the wicked? Read Matthew 25:41-46; Mark 9:42-48; Luke 16:19-31; John 3:36.

3. Read Job 23:1-7; 27:1-6. Did Job harbour ill feelings towards God? What realization moved Job away from such feelings? Read Job 42:1-6.

THE GUIDE

CHAPTER FIVE

COMFORT FOR THE DISCOURAGED

LOOK IT UP

Suggested reading: Psalm 107:35-43

BIBLE REFERENCE

The poor and needy seek water, but there is none,
Their tongues fail for thirst.
I, the LORD, will hear them;
I, the God of Israel, will not forsake them.
I will open rivers in desolate heights,
And fountains in the midst of the valleys;
I will make the wilderness a pool of water,
And the dry land springs of water.
I will plant in the wilderness the cedar
and the acacia tree,
The myrtle and the oil tree;
I will set in the desert the cypress tree and the pine
And the box tree together,
That they may see and know,
And consider and understand together,
That the hand of the LORD has done this,
And the Holy One of Israel has created it
(Isaiah 41:17-20).

INTRODUCTION

A truth capsule

This passage in Isaiah looks forward to that time when the people of God would learn that their captivity was finally over. What an exhilarating and exciting time it would be! But the initial excitement the people would feel upon hearing the announcement would soon give way to anxiety. By the time the announcement would come, the people would have become fairly comfortable in Babylon, and the announcement would mean they would be uprooted again.

The journey itself would pose a substantial problem. Much of it would consist of desert land where there would be no water to drink and no trees for shade. On the other hand, there would be an abundance of wild beasts and thieves. It was a treacherous journey.

The task awaiting them back in their homeland also posed a massive problem. There was no city awaiting them there. There was no city wall. There was no temple. There were no houses. All had to be rebuilt. It was not a matter of them walking up to their front doors, inserting their keys and sitting down in their rooms. As the people considered these things, they would undoubtedly begin to feel discouraged.

THINK ABOUT IT

Some portions of the Bible are especially rich in comfort. Chapters 40-66 of Isaiah's prophecy are some of the most comforting to be found in the Bible. This section begins with these words:

'Comfort, yes, comfort my people!'
    Says your God.
'Speak comfort to Jerusalem,
    and cry out to her...'
                                    (Isaiah 40:1-2).

THINK ABOUT IT

In these chapters, the prophet Isaiah gives the people of Judah a preview of the glorious future awaiting them. Their immediate future was bleak indeed. The Babylonians were going to invade their land, devastate it and carry most of them into captivity. The comforting nature of chapters 40-66 comes largely from the fact that they can look to the end of that captivity and to the rebuilding of Judah.

Chapter 41 is filled with comfort, but provides such comfort for us in one point in particular, that is, in the challenges for which we seem to have no resources.

Some points to ponder

It must have seemed to God's people that they were being called to face an insurmountable challenge and to do so without any of the necessary resources. If we could propel ourselves through time and talk to these released captives about their future, we would perhaps find them likening their situation to wandering through a desert with no water to drink and no trees for shade. A desert poses a huge challenge, but it can be faced if these two essential commodities are available. The future to these released captives, however, seemed to be like facing a desert without either water or shade (v. 17).

A promise

The Lord spoke to his people about the challenge they were facing. Essentially he says, 'Am I to understand that you, my people, look upon your future as being impossible, that you view it in terms of going through a desert where there is no water and no shade? Let me tell you this: I, the Lord your God, am greater than that bleak future. If that future is like a desert, do not let it concern you. I am able to make water flow in the desert and trees spring up everywhere.' He was assuring his people that he was sufficient for them, no matter how meagre their resources.

The angel Gabriel came to Mary with the news that she would bear a son who would be conceived without a human father. Mary responded: 'How can this be?' And Gabriel said, 'For with God nothing will be impossible' (Luke 1:37).

The apostle Paul faced a challenge that appeared to be too much for him: a painful thorn in the flesh. Three times he pleaded with the Lord to remove it, and the Lord said, 'My grace is sufficient for you, for my strength is made perfect in weakness' (2 Corinthians 12:9).

God has the strength we need to face our challenges. When our resources are limited and meagre, his are more than sufficient.

> He giveth more grace when the burdens grow greater;
> He giveth more strength when the labours increase.
> To added affliction He addeth His mercy,
> To multiplied trials His multiplied peace.

EXPLANATION

When we have exhausted our store of
   endurance,
When our strength has failed ere the day is
   half day,
When we reach the end of our hoarded
   resources,
Our Father's full giving has only begun.

His love has no limit; His grace has no measure;
His pow'r has no boundary known unto men.
For out of His infinite riches in Jesus
He giveth, and giveth, and giveth again.[1]

                      (Annie Johnson Flint)

A requirement

It is good to know that God has the strength we
need to face life's challenges. But how do we get
his strength to flow from his unlimited supply
into the little receptacle of our lives? The answer
is given in these words: 'The poor and needy seek
water...' (v. 17).

The water represents the sufficiency of God.
How do we receive it? When we become poor
and needy! When we come to the end of our own
strength! We must come to God admitting that
we do not have the resources for the challenges
and ask him to give us his strength.

Why does God want us to become poor and
needy? Because he wants us to know when he

blesses us that the glory belongs to him, and if we were not poor and needy, we would be trying to take some of the glory for ourselves.

The promise God made to the people would not apply apart from them feeling the enormity of their need (v. 17) and looking to the Lord with the faith and expectation that he would meet their need. The phrase 'I, the LORD, will hear them' (v. 17) assumes that the people would be talking to the Lord about their great need and asking him to meet it.

Here, then, is the word of comfort for the individual saint who is facing enormous challenges: God will be everything you need if you will become 'poor and needy' and seek him. He may not take the problem away. He did not lift the returning captives over the desert and set them down in their homeland. He did not cause their cities and houses to rise magically from the dust. But he did give them strength both for the journey and for the task of rebuilding. In the same way, the Lord will be a strength to us if we will but come to him and ask him.

THINK ABOUT IT

The modern-day church often appears to be living in a waterless, treeless desert. Her opposition often appears to be so very strong and she herself often appears to be so very weak. Many in the church find themselves wringing their hands and saying,

'How are we to face such a time? The challenges are too much for us.'

What is the answer for the church as she faces this age of hostility and abounding wickedness? Is it some new program or promotion? No, the church needs her God to rise up and show himself strong on her behalf. God never does that until he makes his people poor and needy, until they fall on their faces before him and say, 'O God, we are not sufficient to face this hour!'

REMEMBER THIS

Those who have not come to Christ are heading towards a meeting with God who is the holy judge of all the earth. Whether they believe it or not, a day is coming in which they must stand before this God who is ablaze with indignation against sinners. This is a meeting for which they have absolutely no resources. How can sinners ever hope to stand in the presence of a holy God? Some think they will stand there on the basis of their good works, but those works will crumble and disintegrate before their eyes. This holy God demands one hundred per cent righteousness. What are our few good works before such a withering demand? What good is a pound coin if the bill is a billion pounds?

Thank God, there is a word of comfort for un- believers. There is one who has the righteousness that this holy God demands, and that is his Son, Jesus Christ. That righteousness is given to those who become poor and needy, those who come to God saying, 'O God, I cannot stand before your throne. I have no resources. I cast myself upon the infinite resources of Jesus Christ, his perfect life and his atoning death.'

Those who will cast themselves upon the Lord Jesus Christ will find that he will become every- thing they need for their appointment with God. He will forgive them of their sins and grant them eternal life.

QUESTIONS FOR DISCUSSION

1. Deuteronomy 1:19-46 relates a time when the people of Israel became fearful and discouraged. Can you name this episode? What resulted from their discouragement?

2. Read Joshua 1:1-9. What gigantic task was Joshua facing when the Lord told him not to be discouraged?

3. Read 1 Kings 19. Why was Elijah discouraged? How did the Lord encourage him?

THE GUIDE

CHAPTER SIX

COMFORT FOR THE DOUBTING

LOOK IT UP

BIBLE **REFERENCE**

' ... I know whom I have believed and am persuaded
that he is able to keep what I have committed to him
until that day'
(2 Timothy 1:12).

'These things I have written to you who believe in the
name of the Son of God, that you may know that you
have eternal life, and that you may continue to believe
in the name of the Son of God'
(1 John 5:13).

Suggested reading: Romans 8:31-39

INTRODUCTION

A truth capsule

There are three possibilities on the matter of
assurance. We can be saved and not assured. We
can be unsaved but assured. Or we can be both
saved and assured. The Bible would have us to
be the latter, to go rejoicing on our way in the
knowledge that we are secure in him.

Some points to ponder

The testimony of Paul

In the first of these verses, the apostle Paul thun-
ders with triumphant certainty: '...I know whom

I have believed and am persuaded that he is able to keep what I have committed to him until that day.'

Paul was in no doubt about his relationship with the Lord. Even though he had been a vile and wretched sinner, so much so that he called himself the chief of sinners (1 Timothy 1:15), he knew without any shadow of doubt that he had been forgiven of his sin and adopted into the family of God.

The fierce, driving desire of Paul's life was to one day stand acceptably before God. This man had done what so many today refuse to do. He had looked ahead to the end of this life and had seen 'that day' looming in the distance. What day was he talking about? The day of judgement.

Many today will do anything to avoid looking at that day. But Paul had looked at it. It had dominated his thinking. He could not get away from it. As he contemplated it, the question that surged to the forefront of his mind was how he could stand there without fear of being condemned. In other words, Paul wondered where he could safely 'deposit' his hope for that future day.

For a while, it seemed to him that he must depend on his religious heritage and on doing as many good works as possible (Philippians 3:4-6), and he pursued this course with a vigour that was unsurpassed.

That seemed to satisfy Paul for a considerable time. Then one day as he was travelling on the road to Damascus, God intercepted him, knocked him to the ground, blinded his eyes and called out his name. Through God's gracious work in his mind and heart, Paul then realized that he had been depositing his hope for that future day in the wrong place. He came to understand that God is perfect in righteousness, that heaven is a perfect place, and that if he, Paul, were to stand before God acceptably he must be as righteous as God is.

All his hopes and dreams were completely dashed because, even though he was considered to be a very righteous man by all who knew him, he did not have the kind of righteousness that God demanded. That kind of righteousness was so thorough-going, so radical, that it went all the way to the heart itself.

Paul could not live up to that demand for inner righteousness. While he could go down the list of commandments and tick them all off as far as external obedience was concerned, he realized that he had broken them all in his heart (Romans 7:7-9).

Deep, dark despair seized Paul's soul. Was there no place at all where he could safely deposit his hope for that future day? How could he ever live up to God's demand for a perfect righteousness that went all the way to the heart?

Yet God enabled Paul to see that there was one who had the kind of righteousness God demands, the Lord Jesus Christ himself. Paul also came to understand that the righteousness of Christ could be his if he would renounce all other hopes for meeting God's demands and rely completely on Christ.

Now, as he writes to Timothy, Paul is rejoicing because all those years ago he had deposited all his hope for that future day, not in his own doing, but in the work of the Lord Jesus Christ. There was no longer any doubt at all in Paul's mind about that future day. He knew the Lord Jesus Christ, in whom he had deposited all his hope, would not fail to keep that deposit.

He was, therefore, able to say 'I know' and 'I am persuaded'. His hope was not in his good works, in the strength of his faith, or in the emotion he felt when he was saved, or the emotion he had felt since then. All Paul's hope rested in Christ.

The central issue

My first word to those who are struggling with doubt is this: Where have you made your deposit for that awesome day of judgement? What are you depending on? Would it ever occur to you to depend on good works? Would it ever occur to you to depend on your church membership? Would it ever occur to you to depend on the religious heritage of your family?

Everyone who is truly saved has no problem at all in answering these questions. A true Christian may be in the clutches of serious doubt, but he will always answer by pointing to Christ and Christ alone as the only possible hope for salvation.

Satan, of course, tries to get us to look away from Christ as the ground of our hope. If he cannot keep us from going to heaven, he will at least try to make us go

EXPLANATION

there without rejoicing along the way. Satan knows that a doubting Christian is a miserable specimen. He is a poor recommendation of the Christian faith to unbelievers, and is so consumed with doubt that he is able to contribute very little to the work of Christ's kingdom.

So Satan is ever trying to shift the ground of our hope from Christ to something else. If you are not on your guard, he will shift it to your experience and will tell you it is impossible for you to be saved because you were not emotional enough. He will shift it to your performance and convince you that because your behaviour is not what it ought to be, then you could not possibly be a Christian. There is no end to his devices.

But the wise Christian will not allow Satan to shift the ground of his hope. He will always point to the Lord Jesus Christ and his finished work on Calvary's cross, and say to Satan, 'Find some fault in that, and then I will doubt!' How Satan flees when we take our refuge in the mighty Saviour and rub his nose in Calvary's love!

Three tests

The second of our two texts comes from the apostle John. Here John tells us that his purpose in writing his first epistle was in order that his readers might know they have eternal life.

John himself had the same triumphant certainty about his salvation that Paul expressed to Timothy. John expresses his assurance in these words: '...and truly our fellowship is with the Father and with his Son Jesus Christ' (1 John 1:3).

He wanted his readers, then, to share the certainty, the assurance, that he himself knew. To enable them to do so, John gave them three tests.

THINK ABOUT IT

An elderly Scottish lady who was near death was asked by her pastor: 'Sadie, suppose when you die God should allow you to perish. What then?'

She replied in this way: 'If he allows me to perish, He will lose more than I; for though I will lose my soul, He will lose His honor, for He has promised me in His Word, "He that believeth in me shall never die."'[1]

1. The confession test

The first test is what we may refer to as the confession test. In this test John points his readers to the very same thing we noted in the words of Paul. In other words, he points them to Christ as the ground of their hope.

'Do you want to know if you are truly saved?' he seems to ask. Then he answers in this way: 'What do you believe about Jesus Christ? Surely you know what you believe about him! If you can say Christ is the ground of your hope, all is well.' Here it is in John's own words: 'Whoever confesses that Jesus is the Son of God, God abides in him, and he in God' (4:15).

But John does not leave it there. He seems to anticipate his readers asking this question: 'How do we know that we are truly trusting Christ as the ground of our hope?' Then he proceeds to give his readers two more tests.

2. The commandment test

The commandment test is stated by John in these words: 'Now by this we know that we know him, if we keep his commandments. He who says, "I know him," and does not keep his commandments, is a liar, and the truth is not in him' (2:3-4, see also 5:2-3).

No Christian perfectly keeps all the commandments of God. John's point is rather that the child of God takes the commandments of God very seriously. He affirms them as being good and right, he desires and seeks to keep them, and when he fails to do so he is troubled and miserable until he finally comes to repentance.

3. The love test

Then comes what we may refer to as the love test. John describes it as follows: 'We know that we have passed from death to life, because we love the brethren. He who does not love his brother abides in death' (3:14, see also 2:9-11). John's logic on this point is irrefutable. He says, 'If someone says, "I love God," and hates his brother, he is a liar; for he who does not love his brother whom he has seen, how can he love God whom he has not seen?' (4:20).

He was referring, of course, to the words of the Lord Jesus on the night before he was crucified: 'By this all will know that you are my disciples, if you have love for one another' (John 13:35).

What does it mean to love our brothers and sisters in Christ? It certainly means to minister to them in time of need. It must surely include forgiving them when they offend us. It obviously means desiring to be with them in the house of God. In fact, one of the best anti-dotes for doubt is regular worship in the house of God!

THINK ABOUT IT

Blind hymn-writer Fanny J. Crosby often wrote her songs by composing words for an existing tune. After playing for her a tune she had composed, one of her friends asked: 'What does this tune say?' Crosby immediately replied:

Blessed assurance, Jesus is mine!
Oh, what a foretaste of glory divine!
Heir of salvation, purchase of God,
Born of His Spirit, washed in His blood.[2]

Some argue that the ground for assurance is being able to identify the exact time and place where they were saved, but the apostle John does not mention this. As far as he was concerned, present evidence was far more important than past experience. American humorist Will Rogers did not know the date of his birth. When he applied for a passport, he was asked to produce a birth certificate. When Rogers asked why it was needed, the government official replied: 'As a proof of your birth.' Rogers replied: 'I am here, ain't I?'[3]

QUESTIONS FOR DISCUSSION

1. Matthew 7:21-23 gives an example of being assured but not being saved. What will these people plead as the basis for their salvation? What will the Lord Jesus say to them?

2. Read Romans 8:16. What type of assurance does Paul mention here? Are we to expect this type of assurance if the evidences mentioned by John are missing from our lives?

3. Read 2 Peter 1:5-11. What does the Apostle say about making our 'calling and election sure'?

THE GUIDE

CHAPTER SEVEN

COMFORT FOR THE BACKSLIDDEN

LOOK IT UP

'A voice was heard on the desolate heights,
Weeping and supplications of the children of Israel.
For they have perverted their way;
And they have forgotten the LORD their God.
"Return, you backsliding children,
And I will heal your backslidings"'
(Jeremiah 3:21-22).

Suggested reading: Psalm 51

A truth capsule

INTRODUCTION

God's people can and do backslide. By not constantly guarding their hearts against the wiles of the devil, they can slip into sinful living, half-hearted serving and casual worshipping.

The people of Jeremiah's day stand as a prime example of those in a backslidden condition. There was a time when they delighted in the Lord and in keeping his commandments. But they had forgotten (3:21) and forsaken the Lord (2:13, 17, 19). Idolatry and immorality flourished throughout the land while false prophets assured the people that there was nothing to fear from their ungodly lifestyle.

It may be said that the very essence of religion is to be face to face with God. This implies close, intimate fellowship. But in Jeremiah's time the people had turned their backs on God (2:27; 32:33).

THINK ABOUT IT

In 1956 Princess Elizabeth, the widow of the beloved King Albert of Belgium, visited Soviet-dominated Warsaw. A chief of protocol was assigned to accompany her to church one Sunday. When she asked if he was a Christian, he replied: 'Believing, but not practising.' When she asked if he was a Communist, he replied: 'Practising, but not believing.'[1]

When our practice is out of keeping with our profession, we can conclude that we have never truly come to Christ or that we are backslidden.

Some points to ponder

The Lord responded to this sad state of affairs by sending Jeremiah to the people. Jeremiah did not mince his words. He openly addressed the people as 'backsliding Israel' (3:6, 8, 11, 12) and 'backsliding children' (3:14, 22). But he also came with good news that the Lord heals backsliders (3:22). How great was his mercy and grace towards them! It not only made them his people, but it also refused to let them go!

That same grace is still at work today. It is still calling a people out of sin to serve God, and when those people backslide, it still says, 'I will heal your backslidings.' How does this healing take place? The prophecy of Jeremiah presents the answer in a word

that appears forty-five times in this prophecy —
return!

THINK ABOUT IT

The best loved of Jesus' parables is about
returning. The prodigal son, who demanded his share of his father's estate and
spent it in reckless living, came to his
senses and returned to his father. The
father gladly received him. A more fitting
name for the parable of the prodigal son
would be 'The parable of the welcoming
arms'. The father in the parable represents
God. He is truly the God of welcoming
arms. King David strayed, and God welcomed him back. Jonah failed, and God
welcomed him back. Simon Peter denied,
and Christ welcomed him back.

'Return' is a two-sided word. It means we must
come away from where we are and go back to
where we were. It means we once occupied a
certain place, we left it, and we now go back to
occupy it again.

Jeremiah's people had once occupied the
ground of close fellowship with God, but they
had left that behind and were now indulging in
idolatry. They were worshipping what the Bible
calls 'abominations' (4:1). An abomination is

something that is detestable or vile, something that deserves loathing. What an incredible thing! These people had turned their backs on the beauty of God to embrace that which was ugly and vile. In doing so, they had brought nothing but trouble upon themselves. We always invite trouble when we turn from God to embrace false gods.

If they were to experience the blessing of God, they must now forsake their false gods and return to the true God. The solution to their problem, then, was to return to the Lord.

But what does it mean to return to the Lord? Jeremiah's prophecy enables us to understand it as wholeheartedly acknowledging our sin, radically breaking with it, and walking eagerly in the ways of God again.

Acknowledging sin

First, sin must be acknowledged (3:13). To acknowledge sin means we stop excusing and defending it and join with God in condemning and renouncing it.

While we are in a backslidden condition, we are, as it were, on one side of the fence, and God is on the other. We are at odds with him. He speaks to us about our sin, and we begin to offer our excuses. As long as we are doing this, we are still on the path away from God instead of on the path back to him. Healing begins when we take God's side against ourselves. We stop arguing our case against him, and argue his case against ourselves. We agree with him about our sin.

EXPLANATION

Breaking with sin

The next element is breaking radically with our sin. God's message to Jeremiah's generation was crystal clear: 'Put away your abominations out of my sight' (4:1).

We have a tendency to ask God to 'take away' our sins, but God says we are to 'put away' our sins. We have to be ruthless at this point. If going to a particular place tempts us to sin, we must stop going there. If being with some person tempts us to sin, we must cease keeping company with him. Jesus himself said, 'If your right eye causes you to sin, pluck it out and cast it from you... And if your right hand causes you to sin, cut it off and cast it from you...' (Matthew 5:29-30). Jesus was not suggesting that we actually mutilate our bodies. He used this terminology to drive home the truth that sin is so serious that we must take whatever measures are necessary to eliminate it from our lives.

If we were diagnosed with a malignant tumour, we would expect our doctor to remove it. But suppose he said, 'I am going to treat your malignancy by putting a Band-Aid on it.' We would run from his office to a doctor who appreciated the seriousness of the problem.

Sin is to our spiritual well-being what the malignancy is to our physical well-being, and it demands removal. How many of us try to cover it with a Band-Aid!

Later in this prophecy, the Lord uses the phrase, 'Amend your ways and your doings' (Jeremiah 7:3). There is no true repentance apart from changing our ways. Repentance means we do an about-turn. We backslide when we turn from God to sinful thinking and doing. Repentance means we turn back to God. Our faces are towards sin and our backs towards God. Repentance means we turn our faces back towards God and away from sin.

Walking in the ways of the Lord

That, of course, leads to the final point, which is walking eagerly in the ways of God again. This is dealt with in Jeremiah 6:16. Here God's people are urged to look at all the ways available to them, to choose the tried and true way of obedience to God, and to walk faithfully in that way.

There is a great promise attached to this appeal, namely, that they would find rest for their souls. The ways of sin always promise much, but all they ultimately deliver is heartache and ruin.

Jeremiah's prescription is not an easy one. It calls for serious, even painful, heartwork. Jeremiah likens the hearts of the people to ground that has been left unploughed and is now overgrown with weeds and thorns (4:3). Returning to God meant the plough of repentance had to rip through that undisturbed soil. Painful work!

Jeremiah further likens repentance to circumcision (4:4). This physical procedure was selected by God as the sign of the covenant between himself and his chosen people. It was painful work, just as returning to God is.

REMEMBER THIS

We would like to read that Jeremiah's message was well received, that the people saw their sinfulness, heard God's promise to heal them and returned to him with all their hearts. But, alas, this was not the case. Jeremiah sadly says to the Lord, '...they have refused to receive correction. They have made their faces harder than rock; they have refused to return' (Jeremiah 5:3).

What does it mean when God's people hear about their backsliding, hear God's promise to heal it and refuse to break with it? Jeremiah's prophecy resoundingly answers that question. His people continued their backsliding until God rained calamity upon them. The nation of Babylon came in, destroyed the city of Jerusalem and carried most of the people away captive for a period of seventy years. There in Babylon the people finally did what they had refused to do under Jeremiah's ministry. There they returned to God.

The message is loud and clear: God will heal the backsliding of his people through the ministry of his Word or the chastisement of his hand.

QUESTIONS FOR DISCUSSION

1. Read Proverbs 14:14; and Jeremiah 17:13. What consequences of backsliding do these verses mention?

2. Read Psalm 106:7; Isaiah 1:2; Jeremiah 2:31; Hosea 11:1-3; and Micah 6:3-4. On the basis of these verses, what would you select as the most shocking aspect of backsliding?

3. Read Psalm 34:14, 18; 51:17; 147:3. What do these Scriptures say about the Lord's response to true repentance?

CHAPTER EIGHT

COMFORT FOR THE DISAPPOINTED

BIBLE REFERENCE

Can flavourless food be eaten without salt?
Or is there any taste in the white of an egg?
(Job 6:6).

Suggested reading: Habakkuk 3:17-19

INTRODUCTION

A truth capsule

Has it ever occurred to you that each day is something like eating a meal? Some days life places on our plates some very tasty morsels and delicacies, and we are delighted and excited. Other days it places before us common but satisfying fare. These are the meat and potato days. And while we are not exhilarated by these things, we eat and are satisfied.

Then there are those days when the only thing we find on the plate of life is the white of an egg. And it seems there is not so much as a single grain of salt in the salt shaker. These are the days in which our circumstances run against us, as they did with Job, and all the excitement and joy of life evaporate before our eyes. In such times life can become very bland and even repulsive. Welcome to the white of the egg.

Some points to ponder

We are familiar with the story of Job. Within a very short space of time, he went from being a very prosperous man with robust health and a wonderful family to being impoverished, sickly and childless (1:13-19; 2:7-8).

Shortly after these calamities befell him, three of his friends gathered around him to offer their explanations for all this devastation. In their presence Job unleashed his complaints about his suffering. As he did so, he realized that his friends might reproach him. By raising a series of questions, Job insisted that he had a perfect right to complain. Does a wild donkey bray when it has grass? Of course not. Does an ox low if it has fodder? Not likely. Can flavourless food be eaten without salt? Not easily. Is there any taste in the white of an egg? No.

Through these questions, Job was essentially asking: 'Would I be complaining if I had no reason?' As far as Job was concerned, the answer was the same as it was for all the other questions. He would not have been complaining unless there was a good reason, any more than an animal would be complaining if it had plenty to eat.

To Job, his whole life had been reduced to the tasteless white of an egg, and he had, therefore, a perfectly legitimate right to complain. What do we do when life serves up a heaped portion of egg whites?

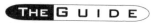
EXPLANATION

Refrain from pronouncing

First, we must refrain from pronouncing too quickly on what life has put on our plate. We all have a tendency to think life is like the white of an egg when, in fact, it is far from it. If we were being candid, most of us would have to admit that there is much that makes our lives worthwhile and happy. Yes, we have our problems; but we also have many, many blessings.

Why do we have this terrible tendency to look right past our blessings, see nothing but our problems and pronounce our lives to be distasteful and loathsome? One of the reasons is that we rather enjoy being the victim. It brings us attention. If we are constantly dining on egg whites, everyone feels sorry for us.

We are also able to talk about ourselves. There are certain things that are off limits when it comes to the matter of talking about ourselves. We cannot talk about our accomplishments for fear of being called proud and self-centred. But if we talk about our problems, no one will say a word. Being a 'victim' also allows us to feel justified in not doing anything for anyone else because we have so many problems of our own.

In this age in which victimhood can be almost 'celebrated' we must be very careful about misrepresenting our lives. Most of us have an egg white or two on our plate, but we also have some very tasty portions.

Remember the good days

Secondly, when life seems to be nothing but the white of an egg, we need to remember with thanksgiving all those days in which we had far more than the white of an egg.

When life's circumstances begin to turn sour, we have a tendency to sour right along with them. And when we begin to sour, we lose our perspective on life. We can even get to the point where we think all of life has been difficult and trying, when, in fact, the majority of our life has been, for most of us, remarkably free of adversity. We must remind ourselves constantly not to let a few bad days obscure the good.

THINK ABOUT IT

Much of our happiness depends on what we choose to dwell on. The apostle Paul was in prison when he wrote his letter to the Philippians. Prison life in his time was a very difficult and depressing existence. But looking at how his imprisonment was furthering the cause of Christ (1:12-18) and on what he had found in Christ (3:1-21), Paul was able to write: 'Rejoice in the Lord always. Again I will say, rejoice!' (4:4).

Remember God

Thirdly, we need to acknowledge that if we *do* have the white of an egg on our plate, it is not there by accident. God placed it there and he has a purpose in doing so. We always want God to explain his purpose in giving us the white of an egg. Sometimes he does, and sometimes he does not.

Job never received the full and final explanation he wanted for having to endure such hardship. But he came to realize that God is God and he owes no one an explanation for what he chooses to do in a person's life.

Joseph, on the other hand, came to understand his adversity. For a long time he must have felt as if his whole life was one gigantic egg white, but he was able to say finally to his brothers who had so cruelly mistreated him: '...you meant evil against me; but God meant it for good, in order to bring it about as it is this day, to save many people alive' (Genesis 50:20).

We do not know now whether we will understand our difficulties in this life, but we know we will understand them all in eternity. And when we finally understand we will be compelled to say our Lord has done all things well — even when he put the white of an egg on our plates.

Remember the salt

A fourth lesson for us to remember is that there is always some salt on the table for the children of God. When the egg white is set before us it

EXPLANATION

seems that there is no salt at all; but a closer look will reveal that there is.

In other words, the Christian always has resources for facing the trials and difficulties of life. The Word of God is a resource, where we read of a heavenly Father who loves us and has our best interests at heart.

The house of God is also a resource. There we meet with God and find strength for living, and there we find our brothers and sisters in Christ who care for us. Now, there is salt for your egg white!

Prayer is another resource. No matter how difficult our circumstances, we can go to the Lord in prayer with the confidence that he hears and cares, and when we pray to him we invariably find ourselves strengthened.

Yet another resource is the cross of Christ. Pondering what the Lord Jesus did there for his people fills the heart with gratitude and causes the problems of life to shrink.

Refrain from harmful seasoning

This brings us to the next lesson. When we are dining on the white of an egg it is extremely important to refrain from seasoning it with something that is harmful. When our circumstances become difficult we are tempted to seek relief as soon as possible. Ours is a day in which there is no shortage of teachings that offer relief, but not all teachings are of God (1 John 4:1). Those who rush out and scoop up teachings that are contrary to the Word of God will ultimately find they would

have been better off to just have eaten their egg white!

THINK ABOUT IT

The apostle Peter devotes a large portion of his second letter to warning his readers about false teachers. In describing these teachers, he mentions the subtle manner in which they come into the church, and the tremendous havoc they create there, teaching 'destructive heresies' (2:1). These teachings are so dangerous that they lead to eternal destruction! False teachers in every age stand as a lasting reminder that it is possible to go a long way in religion and not be truly converted to Christ.

REMEMBER THIS

The children of God will not dine on egg whites for ever. The Bible tells us that a glorious day is coming for the children of God. When that day dawns all the difficulties and sorrows of life will be gone. Egg whites will be removed for ever from the menu. Instead we will dine on the delicacies that the Lord has reserved for those who know and love him.

These days may find many of us in great difficulties. No, they do not begin to compare with Job's, but we still find them to be very trying. We can, like Job, use our circumstances to justify complaining. Or we can look at our difficulties through the lens of Scripture, and in the midst of them be truly thankful to God.

QUESTIONS FOR DISCUSSION

1. Read Acts 16:6-10. Paul may very well have been disappointed when he was not allowed to go into Asia. But the Lord had other purposes for him. How did he make these purposes known? What were some of the results of the Lord leading Paul into Europe? Read Acts 16:11 - 20:6.

2. Read 2 Corinthians 12:7-10. What vital truth did Paul learn that enabled him to cope with the disappointment of having a 'thorn in the flesh'? Read Romans 8:28. Are our disappointments included in the 'all things' of this verse?

3. Read Genesis 29:15-35; and 30:17-20. Was Jacob's disappointment in being forced to marry Leah transformed? How many of his sons did she bear? What special significance is attached to her son Judah? Read Genesis 49:8-12.

CHAPTER NINE

COMFORT FOR THOSE WITH WAYWARD CHILDREN

LOOK IT UP

BIBLE REFERENCE

He who begets a scoffer does so to his sorrow,
And the father of a fool has no joy...
A foolish son is a grief to his father,
And bitterness to her who bore him
(Proverbs 17:21, 25).

Suggested reading: Luke 15:11-24

A truth capsule

INTRODUCTION

There are some parents who, if they felt completely free to confess what they feel in their innermost beings, would say, 'I wish my child had never been born.'

Their happiness over that child has evaporated, and all they feel now is heartache and regret. It may be drinking, drug abuse, spending their time with the wrong crowd, vulgar language, or sexual immorality. It may be lying and stealing. It may be losing their temper at the slightest suggestion of correction or instruction. It may be stubbornly refusing to go to church. Or it may be a combination of all these things.

There is good news for parents who have such anguish. There is help in the Bible. Several passages deal with the matter of child-rearing, but no book has more to say about it than the book of Proverbs. Its teaching is not concentrated in one single passage but is spread throughout the book.

THINK ABOUT IT

The people of Israel probably made use of proverbs from the earliest years of their history. Part of the covenant responsibility of the people of God was to see to it that their children had proper religious training (Deuteronomy 6:4-9). Proverbs came to be used in the process of this training.

When King Solomon came to the throne of Israel, there were already a great number of these proverbs in existence. He gathered them into a collection and added several hundred of his own. Some believe he also set up special schools for the religious training of young men and that his collection of proverbs was used in those schools.

What are proverbs? Someone has defined them as 'short statements drawn from long experiences'. A proverb is really a verbal short cut. It comes from the Latin word *proverba*. *Pro* means 'for', and *verba* means 'words'. A proverb means, then, 'for or in the place of words'.

Some points to ponder

Solomon, the author of the book of Proverbs, was well aware of the very vexing burden of the rebellious child, and he addressed many of his proverbs to it. His favourite word for the rebellious child is not very complimentary. He calls him a 'fool'.

THINK ABOUT IT

THINK ABOUT IT

There are actually three Hebrew words that are translated 'fool' in our Bible. One is *kesil*. It refers to one who makes choices on the basis of what provides immediate pleasure, choices that ultimately lead to ruin. The *kesil* is one who is mentally dull, morally insensitive, arrogant, disrespectful, deceitful and untrustworthy.

The word *ewil* is very close to *kesil*, but it is used for someone who is even worse. It stresses spiritual and moral stupidity. *Nabal* carries the idea of insensitivity to the Lord, moral apathy, and rejecting what is reasonable.[1]

The responsibilities of the child

Solomon addresses the matter of the wayward child by offering some words to that child himself as well as to his parents. His essential message to the child is that he should listen to the instructions of his parents! (1:8; 2:1; 4:1, 20; 5:1; 6:20; 7:1; 13:1; 19:27).

Solomon was not content, however, simply to urge his son to listen to him. He also gave him motives or incentives for doing so.

Parental instructions and guidance have the child's best interest at heart.

Solomon says parental instructions are 'graceful ornaments' on the head. This may mean that the child who follows his parents' instructions becomes a graceful person who is respected by others. Young people, when your parents give you instructions, please keep this in mind. They do so in order that you might be this type of person.

Solomon also describes the instructions of parents as 'life' and 'health' (4:22). That can be taken to mean that the child who listens to his parents finds true joy and happiness in this life. But it also may mean that listening to parental instruction may very well keep a child out of an early grave (3:2).

Young people, heed this word. Parents are not perfect. They do not know everything (although they do know more than their children!), but they love you more than you will ever know and their instructions are designed to bring you happiness, not to spoil it.

That brings me to the second great incentive Solomon uses in his instructions to the young.

Failure to heed parental instruction brings great grief and misery to one's parents (10:1; 15:20; 17:21, 25; 19:13).

A rebellious child takes the happiness completely out of life for his parents. Every single day they live has a

dark cloud hanging over it. There is never a let-up in the heartache they feel. I ask our young people to consider this. Your parents have invested more time, more work, more love, and more money in you than you can believe. Do you really want to repay their investment by destroying their happiness?

The responsibility of the parents

But Solomon also has a great deal to say to parents about this matter of the rebellious child. We can summarize his teaching in two words: train (22:6) and discipline (19:18; 22:15; 23:13-14; 29:15, 17).

Training

Let us consider this matter of training for a moment. Solomon says the training should be with a view to guiding the child 'in the way he should go'. This is surely the way that is opposite to the way the rebellious, foolish youngster is going. It is the way of devotion to God, respect and love for parents, and the way of happiness and fulfilment for the child himself.

Parents themselves must know the proper way for their children to go, be convinced of the rightness of this way, and must model it for their youngsters. We cannot expect our children to

EXPLANATION

show devotion to God if we do not show it ourselves. We cannot expect them to show respect to us if we conduct ourselves in a way that does not deserve respect.

Nothing can replace the positive example of parents. Happy parents who love and serve God, who love and respect each other, and who are clean in life and language will most certainly have a powerful impact for good on their children.

Parents must also begin very early in providing positive instruction regarding this way. It is important to have the child in church on a regular basis, but it is also essential that the parent talks with the child daily about *what* is important in life and *why* it is important. Such private instruction of the child should seek to supplement the teaching of the church by bringing the Christian view of life to bear on every situation.

One of the best ways to provide positive instruction for children is to read good books to them while they are very small and discuss what those books teach.

Discipline

Then there is the matter of discipline. Discipline expresses the love of the parent for the child, love that is so great that it is willing to take unpleasant action in order to help the child to be what he ought to be.

Discipline should never be cruel. It should start early in life, be consistently applied, and always take into account the stage the child is at. It should never be unwilling to hear the child's case and should never be done in anger.

REMEMBER THIS

REMEMBER THIS

Even with the wise application of training and discipline some children still rebel. It is, sadly enough, possible for godly people to have rebellious children. What are parents to do when this is the case?

Solomon would have us cling mightily to this promise — even though our child may depart for a time and rebel against us, the godly training we have given him will follow him. There is, of course, no guarantee that such training will bring our children to faith. This is entirely a matter of God's grace. But there is comfort in knowing that God's grace is great and his will is perfect.

So if you are a parent who has, with all your imperfections and inadequacies, conscientiously tried to train and discipline your child only to see him rebel, hear this word. Do not give up. Continue to love that child. Continue to pray for him, and continue to talk with him. In due time that child may very well cease to break your heart and become a source of tremendous pride and consolation.

QUESTIONS FOR DISCUSSION

1. Read Deuteronomy 6:6-9. What must be true of us before we can teach our children the Word of God? What is the word that summarizes the manner in which we are to teach our children?

2. Read Ephesians 6:1-4. What is the responsibility assigned to children? What promise is given to children who discharge this responsibility? What is the responsibility assigned to fathers?

3. Can you think of some godly fathers in the Bible who failed to rear godly children? Read 1 Samuel 2:12-17; 8:1-3; 2 Samuel 13:1 - 18:33; 1 Kings 1:1-6.

CHAPTER TEN

COMFORT FOR THOSE BRUISED BY DIFFICULT CIRCUMSTANCES

LOOK IT UP

BIBLE REFERENCE

A bruised reed he will not break,
And smoking flax he will not quench,
Till he sends forth justice to victory
(Matthew 12:20).

Suggested reading: John 8:1-12

INTRODUCTION

A truth capsule

The reed in our reference related to a small musical instrument that shepherds would fashion while they were out in the field with their sheep. With these instruments they could amuse and entertain themselves during the long, monotonous hours during which they kept watch. The reed worked very well until it became bruised or cracked, and then it was useless. The smoking flax refers to a candle that is just barely flickering.

Many who know the Lord have to admit that these emblems often represent them. There was a time in which they made beautiful music for the Lord, but now they are bruised reeds. There was a time when they shone brightly for the Lord, but now there is more smoke than light in their lives.

THINK ABOUT IT

The puritan Richard Sibbes wrote *The Bruised Reed and Smoking Flax*. Dr Martyn Lloyd-Jones gave this testimony regarding Sibbes' work: '...Richard Sibbes ... was a balm to my soul at a period in my life when I was overworked and badly overtired, and therefore subject in an unusual manner to the onslaughts of the devil. In that state and condition, to read theology does not help, indeed it may be well-nigh impossible; what you need is some gentle tender treatment for your soul. I found at that time that Richard Sibbes, who was known in London in the early seventeenth century as "The Heavenly Doctor Sibbes" was an unfailing remedy. His books *The Bruised Reed* and *The Soul's Conflict* quietened, soothed, comforted, encouraged and healed me.'[1]

Some points to ponder

Good news

The Lord Jesus Christ, whom we love and serve, is so kind and tender with his people that he understands their frailties and sympathizes with them. He does not break bruised reeds or quench smoking candles. In fact, the Lord Jesus actually restores bruised people. Fanny J. Crosby stated this truth admirably well:

Down in the human heart, crushed by the tempter
Feelings lie buried that grace can restore.
Touched by a loving heart, wakened by kindness,
Chords that are broken will vibrate once more.[2]

THINK ABOUT IT

Fanny J. Crosby was an American hymn-writer who lost her sight when she was only six weeks old. At the age of eleven she enrolled at the New York City Institution for the Blind where she remained for twenty-three years as both a student and teacher.

During her long life (she died in 1915 at age 95), Fanny J. Crosby wrote over two thousand hymns. Some of the best known are: 'To God be the Glory'; 'Redeemed, How I Love to Proclaim It'; 'Rescue the Perishing'; and 'Tell Me the Story of Jesus'.[3]

Simon Peter was very much a bruised reed after Jesus arose from the grave. He had failed the Lord miserably by denying him three times. He undoubtedly felt that he would never again make music for the Lord or shine for him. But the Lord tenderly took his bruised disciple and restored him (John 21).

How does the Lord show his care for his bruised people? Sometimes he draws near and floods them with a sense of his presence. Sometimes he causes a promise from Scripture to 'leap off' the page. Sometimes he uses another saint of God to speak a word of comfort.

A caution

Some eagerly take the tenderness of Jesus to mean that they can live without regard to God or his commands. All who equate the tenderness of Jesus with ambivalence towards him would do well to read this entire passage. While the Lord is tender, he also has a flaming concern for justice. This passage tells us that he not only came to declare justice (v. 18) but that he will also eventually lead justice to victory.

The picture here is of God's justice being cast down into the mud and surrounded by scoffers and revilers. But justice does not stay there. The Lord Jesus comes along, lifts her up and escorts her to a throne where she is seated and all have to submit to her.

Those who reject Christ's tender offer of forgiveness in the gospel will eventually find themselves standing before that enthroned justice! The option presented to us in Scripture is quite simple — accept the tender Saviour now or meet him in eternity as your judge.

A consolation

Through the ministry of the prophet Isaiah, God gave this promise regarding the work of the Messiah:

He will not fail nor be discouraged,
Till he has established justice in the earth
(Isaiah 42:4).

We must not take this to mean that Jesus never knew weakness in his humanity. He, being fully human, knew what it was to experience weariness. And we are told that he died in weakness on the cross (2 Corinthians 13:4). It rather means that while Jesus knew weakness in his flesh, he knew none in his spirit. He was utterly devoted to his Father and to the work that his Father had given him to do.

We are often like cracked reeds and smoking wicks in serving the Lord, but Jesus was neither. Because he never swerved nor wavered in faithfulness to God, his people have eternal salvation.

REMEMBER THIS

REMEMBER THIS

If Jesus is so tender to bruised saints, how tender those saints should be with each other! The apostle Paul writes: 'Brethren, if a man is overtaken in any trespass, you who are spiritual restore such a one in a spirit of gentleness, considering yourself lest you also be tempted. Bear one another's burdens, and so fulfil the law of Christ' (Galatians 6:1-2).

QUESTIONS FOR DISCUSSION

1. *Read John 13:34-35; 1 John 4:7-11. What is the basic disposition that Christians are to have towards each other?*

2. *Read Romans 14:13; 15:7; Galatians 6:2; Ephesians 4:32; 1 Thessalonians 5:11; Hebrews 10:24; James 4:11; 5:16. How is our basic disposition towards our fellow Christians to manifest itself?*

3. *Can you give some examples of Jesus showing tenderness to people?*

CHAPTER ELEVEN

COMFORT FOR THOSE WHO DOUBT GOD'S LOVE

ᐸBIBLE REFERENCEᐳ

The LORD your God in your midst,
The Mighty One, will save;
He will rejoice over you with gladness,
He will quiet you with his love,
He will rejoice over you with singing
(Zephaniah 3:17).

Suggested reading: Isaiah 62:1-5

A truth capsule

The Bible is the account of God speaking. God spoke and this world and the whole universe sprang into existence. As we work our way through the Old Testament, we consistently find God speaking. He spoke to Abraham and Moses, to Joshua and Gideon, to Samuel and David. We find God calling a steady succession of prophets to speak for him. We come to the New Testament and we find the Lord Jesus Christ stepping on the stage of human history. The Lord Jesus came to speak the words of God, and he spoke in such a way that his listeners 'marvelled at the gracious words which proceeded out of his mouth' (Luke 4:22).

We are very familiar, then, with God speaking. But here in Zephaniah we have the prophet promising his people that God would sing over them.

Some points to ponder

The prophecy of Zephaniah is built around two 'days'. The first was the terrible day of God's judgement upon the people of Judah (1:7, 14-16), when the Babylonians would come in to devastate the nation and carry the people away captive.

The second day was the day of restoration when, after seventy years of captivity, the people would be released and brought back to their homeland. Zephaniah was looking at this day when he made reference to God singing.

These words are filled to the brim with breathtaking truths for the people of Judah, and for us as well. God's presence is here. He promised to be in their midst. God's power is here. He, mighty to save, would deliver and protect his people. And God's enjoyment of his people is here. He would 'quiet' them with his love (perhaps this means he would quietly enjoy them as he rested in his love for them). He would rejoice over them with singing.

God singing! Let us explore this a little.

Those over whom God promised to sing

A repentant people

The people of Judah would go into captivity in Babylon because of their sins. Zephaniah mentions in particular their idolatrous worship (1:4-6) and their moral degeneracy (3:1, 3-4). A good summary of the wickedness of

the people is found in the four specific indict-
ments of the second verse of chapter three. The
people of Judah refused to obey God, to receive
correction, to trust God and to draw near to
God.

At this time the Lord did not sing over them
but grieved. In his grief he sent them to Babylon.
There they came to their senses and repented of
their sins, and God began to rejoice over them.
God always rejoices over his people, no matter
how grievous their sin, if they will turn from
those sins and give him the devotion he desires
and deserves. Jesus' parable of the prodigal son
is a New Testament illustration of this truth (Luke
15:11-24).

An imperfect people

While the people of God repented in their captivity, they came back to their homeland as an
imperfect people. All we have to do in order to
see this is to read the post-exilic prophets the
Lord sent to them: Haggai, Zechariah and
Malachi. But the prophecy of Zephaniah makes
a wonderful truth exceedingly plain: the Lord
would sing over them even in their imperfection.

Many Christians are keenly conscious of their
failings. They remember the determination they
had when they first came to know the Lord. They
remember how eager they were to serve him and

EXPLANATION

how fervently they loved him. But with the passing of
time they found their ardour cooling. They now realize that they have not been much in their Bibles or in
prayer. They have not had much concern over the souls
of others. They may even have engaged in a particularly heinous sin.

The truth is that many believers, if asked to convey
how God views them, would never think of him singing over them. They would be more likely to regard
him as a frowning, heavenly policeman who is ready
and eager to bash them with his celestial truncheon.

Let us be clear about this. While God does not excuse the sins of his people, he still sees much in them
that causes him to rejoice. He sees in each of his children one for whom Christ died; and he sings. He sees
one in whom his Spirit operated; and he sings. He sees
one with whom his Spirit even now bears witness and
for whom his Spirit prays; and he sings. He sees one
who, with all his frailty and failings, loves him and
desires to serve him; and he sings. He sees one who
does not himself excuse sin but is troubled by it and
desires to be free from it; and he sings. He sees one
who is touched by the needs of others and desires to
minister to them; and he sings. He sees one who by his
grace will finally come into his presence to share his
glory eternally; and he sings.

There is nothing in and of the Christian himself that
makes God sing over him. But standing on the basis of
the redeeming work of Christ and perfumed by Christ's
ongoing ministry of intercession in heaven, each

Christian is so pleasing to God that he, the Lord, bursts out in song. God does not sing over his people because they are worthy or deserving. He sings over them because they are tokens of his grace. His singing over his people testifies to his own grace that has worked in their lives, the grace that chose them, regenerated them, called them and forgave them.

It is that grace that is now at work in sanctifying his people, and that grace will finally lead them home.

THINK ABOUT IT

THINK ABOUT IT

God the Father takes delight in God the Son. This was true before the foundation of the world. Paul tells us that 'all things were created … for him' (Colossians 1:16). It was true while he was engaged in his earthly ministry, during which God spoke from heaven three times to express his delight (Matthew 3:17; 17:5; John 12:27-28). It is true now in that the Lord Jesus Christ is at the right hand of God to make intercession for all who believe (Mark 16:19; Romans 8:34; Ephesians 1:20; Colossians 3:1).

If God so delights in his Son, he cannot help but delight in those who are covered by the righteousness of his Son.

The appropriate response to God's singing

Joy

Through the prophet the Lord says:

> Sing, O daughter of Zion!
> Shout, O Israel!
> Be glad and rejoice with all your heart,
> O daughter of Jerusalem!
>
> (Zephaniah 3:14).

If God is singing over his people, they have abundant reason to sing. They have reason to rejoice, not half-heartedly and casually, but wholeheartedly and fervently. Alexander Maclaren appropriately writes of this text: 'It becomes us to see to it that our religion is a religion of joy. Our text is an authoritative command as well as a joyful exhortation, and we do not fairly represent the facts of Christian faith if we do not "rejoice in the Lord always". In all the sadness and troubles which necessarily accompany us, as they do all men, we ought by the effort of faith to set the Lord always before us that we be not moved.'[1]

THINK ABOUT IT

Scripture gives a significant amount of attention to singing. God's people are to be a singing people.

They are commanded to sing (Psalm 81:1; 98:1; 105:2; 149:1). They are to emulate Paul who resolved to sing with spirit and understanding (1 Corinthians 14:15). They are not only to sing with their mouths but also to make melody in their hearts to the Lord as a means of giving thanks to him (Ephesians 5:19-20). They cannot sing as they ought if they do not allow the Word of God to dwell 'richly' in them (Colossians 3:16).

> Let those refuse to sing
> Who never knew our God;
> But children of the heavenly King,
> But children of the heavenly King,
> May speak their joys abroad,
> May speak their joys abroad.
> …
>
> Then let our songs abound,
> And every tear be dry;
> We're marching thro' Immanuel's ground,
> We're marching thro' Immanuel's ground,
> To fairer worlds on high,
> To fairer worlds on high.
>
> (Isaac Watts)

Confidence

The Lord also says to his people:

'In that day it shall be said to Jerusalem: "Do not
    fear;
Zion, let not your hands be weak"'

(v. 16).

The phrase 'let not your hands be weak' refers to
letting the hands drop in fear and despair. The Lord
wanted his people to understand that there was no
reason for them to despair. Their sins had not separated them from him. He would still delight in them.

REMEMBER THIS

Believers today are entitled to draw comfort here.
If the Lord has such delight in his people, we can
be sure he is aware of our circumstances and is
present in the midst of them to sustain and help
us. If God is delighted with his people, we can be
sure he will never throw his hands up in despair
over us, but will finally complete his work in us and
bring us to eternal glory. God will never allow himself to be deprived of one single believer because
each one brings him so much joy. Let the devil
rage. If God is singing, his rage does not matter.

QUESTIONS FOR DISCUSSION

1. Read Isaiah 62:1-5 for an additional statement about
    God rejoicing over his people. What does God promise

DISCUSS IT

to call his people? What does he promise to call their land?

2. *Read Psalm 100. What reasons do the people of God have for singing?*

3. *Read John 3:16; Romans 5:8; and 1 John 4:7-11. What indisputably proves the love of God for his people?*

CHAPTER TWELVE

COMFORT FOR THOSE WHO DOUBT GOD'S WORD

LOOK IT UP

'Scripture cannot be broken'
(John 10:35).

Suggested reading: 2 Timothy 3:1-17

INTRODUCTION

A truth capsule

There is no doubt that the Bible claims to be the source of correct information about knowledge of God. But can it be trusted? Is it reliable?

Some say the Bible is a reliable guide to the knowledge of God, but it is not totally reliable. In fact, they say, the Bible has both many and varied errors — scientific errors, historical errors, statistical errors and even theological errors.

I have to say that this kind of talk leaves me feeling distinctly uneasy. If the Bible is filled with errors, how do we know it tells us the truth about this essential matter of knowing God? What if it contains so many incorrect essential details that the whole meaning is changed and distorted?

Most of us would not call a car reliable even if it started nine out of ten times and a Bible that is right on as many as nine out of every ten details would still inspire more doubt than confidence.

> **THINK ABOUT IT**

Accuracy is important. A lady travelling abroad wanted to purchase a very expensive item. She wired her husband for his approval. The husband gave the telegraph operator the following response: 'No. Expense too great.' But the operator mistakenly wired: 'No expense too great.'

The wife gleefully made the purchase — much to the chagrin of her husband and the embarrassment of the telegraph operator![1]

Some issues are so vitally important we just cannot afford to be wrong about them. The knowledge of God is right at the top of the list in this category. If you get the wrong information here you will be lost eternally.

Some points to ponder

Are there substantial and solid reasons for insisting the Bible is totally reliable? Or is this just mere superstition and wishful thinking? Most of us are willing to accept something on the basis of one or two solid evidences. The truth is that there is a tremendously impressive array of reasons for the complete reliability of Scripture.

The testimony of Jesus

The first and foremost reason is that Jesus himself put his stamp of approval upon the whole of Scripture. This

means at least two things. The Old Testament was completed years before Jesus began his earthly ministry, but the writing of the New Testament did not even begin until after his death on the cross. To put his stamp of approval on all of Scripture means, then, that he had to endorse the Old Testament as it existed and to pre-endorse the New Testament.

Endorsement of the Old Testament

EXPLANATION

His endorsement of the Old Testament came in several impressive ways.

His final court of appeal. First, he used it in such a way as to indicate that he regarded it as the final court of appeal. When Satan assaulted him with three dreadfully sinister temptations, Jesus resisted him each time by quoting Scripture (Matthew 4:1-11).

An ongoing feature of Jesus' ministry was frequent and fierce debates with the religious experts of the day. Invariably, Jesus confounded them and won the day by appealing to Scripture. Perhaps the most noteworthy of these confrontations is where Jesus answered the Sadducees' question about the bodily resurrection by appealing to the verb tense of an Old Testament passage (Matthew 22:23-33). That is verbal inspiration with a vengeance!

THINK ABOUT IT

It has been observed that the Sadducees were 'sad, you see' because they did not believe in the resurrection of the dead. Although they were at odds with the Pharisees on this point of doctrine as well as several others, they were united with them in a common dislike for Jesus and a desire to see him discredited. In this quest, the Sadducees posed one of their favourite resurrection riddles. Jesus exposed the root of their scepticism by saying, 'Are you not therefore mistaken, because you do not know the Scriptures nor the power of God?' (Mark 12:24). His analysis applies with equal force to theological liberalism of every age.

His explicit affirmations. Secondly, Jesus explicitly affirmed the complete trustworthiness and reliability of the Old Testament. When he wanted to talk about the certainty of Scripture being fulfilled he selected the smallest characters of the Hebrew alphabet (Matthew 5:17-18). On another occasion, he asserted bluntly: 'Scripture cannot be broken' (John 10:35). What was he saying? Simply that Scripture cannot be demonstrated to be wrong at even one point. The implication is that if Scripture could be proven wrong at one point then the whole would come tumbling to the ground; but Scripture is so sure and reliable such proof is not forthcoming!

EXPLANATION

His endorsement of disputed passages. Thirdly, and perhaps most striking of all, Jesus seemed to go out of his way to affirm those parts of the Old Testament that are most often dismissed as mere myths. Adam and Eve (Matthew 19:4-5), Noah and the Flood (Matthew 24:37-39), the fiery judgement on Sodom and the terrible fate of Lot's wife (Luke 17:28-32), the miraculous ministries of Elijah and Elisha (Luke 4:25-27), and Jonah and the great fish (Matthew 12:39-41) — all were treated by him as indisputable historical facts!

His endorsement of the New Testament

So much for Jesus' endorsement of the Old Testament! What about the New Testament? How could Jesus possibly have endorsed it before it was even written? Because Jesus gave his disciples the assurance that each part of the New Testament's writing would be supervised by the Holy Spirit himself. The New Testament consists of three parts. The Gospels and Acts are historical in nature. Those writers would need accurate recollection of events. The epistles are doctrinal in nature. They are designed to impart instruction and guidance in our believing and behaving. Those writers would need keen insight into the truths of God. Finally, the book of Revelation is prophetic in nature. Its writer would need insight into things to come.

The night before he was crucified, Jesus assured his disciples that the Holy Spirit would provide each of these needed elements. He would call things to their remembrance (John 14:26), he would guide them into truth (John 16:13), and he would even disclose things to come (John 16:13). So no matter where you turn in Scripture you may rest assured Jesus Christ has initialled every page!

Some say Jesus' testimony about Scripture does not count because it amounts to circular reasoning; that is, the Bible tells us about Jesus and Jesus tells us about the Bible. The truth is, however, Jesus has to be considered an authority by virtue of his resurrection from the dead, and that event is confirmed by solid historical evidence (an empty tomb, eyewitnesses, etc.). This Jesus, who is obviously no ordinary man, is the one who endorses Scripture. Doesn't it make sense to accept his evaluation?

Even if the testimony of Jesus is somehow discounted or skirted, Scripture still stands like the Rock of Gibraltar. There are, in other words, several other inescapable evidences that this book is God's book and that it is wholly reliable.

The unity of Scripture

For one thing, the unity of Scripture shows it is no ordinary book. Here is a book that was produced over a period of 1600 years by more than forty writers from many walks of life. Some of it was written by kings

(David and Solomon) and some of it was written by common fishermen (Peter and John). Some of it was written by a scholarly rabbi (Paul), and some of it was written by a tax-collector (Matthew). For all of this, the Bible has only one message — the message of God's gracious redemption for those who repent of their sins and embrace his way of salvation.

Josh McDowell relates his experience with a salesman of the series *Great Books of the Western World*. After listening to his pitch, McDowell asked what the result would be if ten of the authors of this series tried to address just one controversial subject. 'A conglomeration,' the man replied. McDowell proceeded to point out that the forty or so writers of the Bible address hundreds of controversial subjects with perfect harmony. Two days later the man committed himself to Christ.[2]

The fulfilment of prophecy

Another of the strongest indications of the complete reliability of Scripture is its fulfilled prophecies. The Old Testament is filled with prophecies regarding nations and cities, and these prophecies were stunningly fulfilled. Josh McDowell cites several of these along with the statistical probability of their fulfilment in his book, *Evidence That Demands A Verdict*. The greatest prophecies of the Old Testament, however, are those pertaining to the Messiah. Here again, McDowell's book is devastating to the critics. He isolates sixty-one major prophecies of the Old Testament that were minutely fulfilled by Jesus Christ. The statistical probability of one man fulfilling just a mere eight of these prophecies is astronomical, and Jesus fulfilled them all.[3]

In addition to these evidences many more could be cited — the Bible's ability to survive attacks, the changed lives of those who believe and obey it, the inner consciousness that it is a divine book, its correspondence to what we observe in life, the discoveries of archaeologists.

Despite all these evidences, millions refuse to acknowledge the Bible as God's reliable word. Each time an evidence is mentioned they are able to find some way to explain it away. They remind me of someone trying to demonstrate that an avalanche is avoidable because each stone has a certain, defined path. Theoretically, one can avoid an avalanche by merely avoiding each stone. Unfortunately, avalanches do not come at us stone by stone, but all at once.

So it is with the evidences for the Bible. They do not come to us in isolation but together. One evidence may not seem like so much, but the sheer weight of their united witness leaves the perceptive person no alternative but to admit the Bible is indeed the reliable Word of God himself.

The most amazing person, however, is not the hard-nosed sceptic who refuses to admit he has been hit by an avalanche and persists in diagramming the path of each stone. The most amazing is the one who recognizes the avalanche of evidence for the Bible, admits it is God's Word, and refuses to order his life in accordance with it. Yes, there are those who believe the Bible is God's Word but who have never embraced the Saviour it presents as their Lord and Saviour. Even more startling, there are those who say they believe the Bible is God's Word and they have embraced the Saviour, but who feel absolutely no compulsion to heed what God says about how the Christian life is to be lived.

REMEMBER THIS

Tipping the hat to the evidence for the Bible cuts no ice with God. We can say all we want that we believe in the Bible, but in the last analysis, only those who are seriously and diligently trying to live according to the Bible really believe it is God's Word.

QUESTIONS FOR DISCUSSION

1. *What emblems do the biblical authors use to convey the nature of the Word of God? Read*

REMEMBER THIS

Psalm 119:105; Jeremiah 23:29; Matthew 18:18-23; Ephesians 6:17; Hebrews 4:12.

2. *What constitutes a proper response to the Word of God? Read Psalm 119:161; Isaiah 66:2, 5; Jeremiah 15:16; Acts 11:1; 17:11; James 1:22-23.*

3. *Read 1 Kings 22:1-28; Jeremiah 28:1-17. What is the significance of unfulfilled prophecies?*

THE GUIDE

CHAPTER THIRTEEN

COMFORT FOR THOSE WHO ARE TROUBLED BY EVIL

BIBLE REFERENCE

'The field is the world, the good seeds are the sons of the kingdom, but the tares are the sons of the wicked one. The enemy who sowed them is the devil, the harvest is the end of the age, and the reapers are the angels. Therefore as the tares are gathered and burned in the fire, so it will be at the end of this age' (Matthew 13:38-40).

'Again, the kingdom of heaven is like a dragnet that was cast into the sea and gathered some of every kind, which, when it was full, they drew to shore; and they sat down and gathered the good into vessels, but threw the bad away. So it will be at the end of the age. The angels will come forth, separate the wicked from among the just, and cast them into the furnace of fire. There will be wailing and gnashing of teeth' (Matthew 13:47-50).

Suggested reading: Psalm 73

A truth capsule

INTRODUCTION

If God's kingdom has come among us in and through Christ, why is there still so much evil in the world?

We are not the first of Christ's followers to be troubled by that question. Jesus' original twelve disciples were, as well. They knew John the Baptist had preached that the Messiah's coming would be like an axe being laid to the root of every evil tree (Matthew 3:10). They also remembered John saying the Messiah would come with a fan in his hand to blow away the chaff so he could gather his wheat into the barn (Matthew 3:12). These men believed Jesus was the Messiah of whom John had spoken, but they were perplexed. The Messiah was here, but evil was still very much alive and well. If anything, the coming of Jesus had only made evil men, such as the Pharisees, even more evil.

Jesus dealt with the perplexity of his disciples by sharing with them the parable of the tares and the parable of the dragnet. Through these parables Jesus taught his disciples that his coming was not intended to signal the abrupt end of evil. They and the other kingdom citizens were rather to live with evil until the end of the age. Jesus designed these two parables to teach identical truths about this kingdom: the reality of evil in this age and the certainty of judgement in the age to come.

Some points to ponder

The reality of evil

The parable of the tares (Matthew 13:24-30, 36-43)

With this parable Jesus points out the reality of evil in this world. He himself is the sower of the good seed and the field in which he sows is the world. In other words, Christ grows his followers in this world. They are not taken out of the world as soon as they become citizens of his kingdom.

But Christ is not the only sower in this world. There is an 'enemy' (v. 25) who sows, as well. Jesus left no doubt about the identity of this enemy. It is none other than Satan himself (v. 39).

Satan's sowing is totally unlike the Lord's. While the Lord sows good seeds, Satan sows tares. Tares closely resemble the genuine wheat stalks, but they produce no wheat. They appear to be genuine but they are not. They are counterfeits masquerading as the true thing.

We are to understand from this, then, that while our Lord sows true followers in this world, Satan sows phoney, false followers. Christ has in this world his crop of kingdom citizens, and Satan has his crop of counterfeits. It has always been his grand scheme to deceive people by imitating the works of God.

We should not miss the fact that Satan did his sowing 'while men slept' (v. 25). In other words, he does his work clandestinely and deceptively. It was through his deception of Eve that sin was brought into the world in the first place, and it is through this same subtle deception that evil continues to thrive. Paul warns us about 'the wiles of the devil' (Ephesians 6:11). Satan is so wily that Paul says that he is 'transformed into an angel of light' (2 Corinthians 11:14).

Because Satan is ever at work in this world, kingdom citizens are wrong to expect the presence of the kingdom of Christ to eradicate evil in this world. As long as this world exists, there will be evil in it. No matter how much money governments may spend, no matter how thoroughly we commit ourselves to educating our young, no matter how vigorously the church goes about her work, evil will never cease to exist in this world.

The parable of the dragnet (vv. 47-50)

This parable brings before us an even more solemn reality, that is, the existence of evil in the church herself.

The dragnet is cast into the sea. When the fishermen pulled the net to the shore they found that it was full. But because some of the fish were not good, the fishermen were obliged to sort them, keeping the good and discarding the bad.

THINK ABOUT IT

The dragnet, the largest of all fishing nets, had weights attached to the bottom and wooden floats to the top. It was usually put into the water from a boat so workers standing on the shore could pull it through the water with attached ropes. On some occasions it was drawn to shore by the men in the boat.[1]

The net represents the preaching of the gospel, and the fish represent those who seem to be brought into the church through the preaching of the gospel.

There have been many times when the net was full, times in which the gospel had such tremendous appeal that many professed true faith in Christ. But the fact that the net of the gospel is full does not mean that all in the net are truly saved. This phenomenon is particularly true in times of revival. In such times some are moved emotionally by the wonderful things happening around them and they profess faith in Christ. But they are merely caught in the net. They are the bad fish who do not have genuine faith.

The fact that someone professes to be in the kingdom does not mean he is. The church always has had, and always will have, those who still belong to the realm of evil. The coming of Christ's kingdom into this world does not, then, obliterate evil in the world (the tares) or even prevent it from entering into the church itself (the dragnet).

Lest we despair over these realities, let us turn our attention to the second truth driven home by these parables.

The certainty of judgement

The inclination of the sower's servants when the tares were detected was to rush into the field and start uprooting them (v. 28), but the owner of the field insisted that the tares be left until the harvest (vv. 29-30). The harvest represents the end of the age. At that time the Lord will deal with the tares. Jesus describes that time in these words: 'The Son of Man will send out his angels, and they will gather out of his kingdom all things that offend, and those who practise lawlessness, and will cast them into the furnace of fire. There will be wailing and gnashing of teeth' (vv. 41-42).

The parable of the dragnet ends in exactly the same way. The angels will separate the good fish from the bad at the end of the age, and the bad fish, representing the wicked, will be cast into 'the furnace of fire' where there is 'wailing and gnashing of teeth' (vv. 49-50).

The Lord Jesus Christ is not telling us that we should not at this present time stand against evil in the world and in the church. We know we should because many other Scriptures tell us to do so. Government itself has been ordained of God to have a restraining effect on evil in this world. And church discipline is to be exercised for the express purpose of dealing with evil in the midst of the church.

The point is rather that when we have done all we can do to resist evil in this world and in the church, evil will still exist in both. It will never be completely eradicated from either until the end of the age.

Whether we like it or not, this is God's way of dealing with evil. God does not yield to our questioning on this matter. He does not explain to us why evil is not eliminated here and now. Neither does he tell us why some seem to skate through life without feeling the full force of evil, while others seem to catch the brunt of it. His response to our questions about evil is this: 'Wait. I'll take care of it.'

Job, who saw more of evil than any of us ever will, constantly demanded an explanation from God, but he never received it. God essentially said to him, 'Trust me.'

Asaph, the author of Psalm 73, struggled with the very same issue. He saw the wicked flourishing and the righteous languishing. It was almost too much for him. He finally turned the corner when he looked beyond the circumstances of this world to eternity. He says he went into the sanctuary and there 'understood their end' (v. 17). In the house of the Lord he came to understand that the wicked are standing on 'slippery places' and that they will eventually be cast down 'to destruction' (v. 18).

The key to coping with evil in this world is, then, not to look at the here and now where it so often appears that 'truth is for ever on the scaffold, wrong for ever on the throne'. The key is to look at the end when God will finally balance the books and make all things right.

This means the citizens of Christ's kingdom must patiently endure evil until the end comes. It also means those who are not yet citizens of the kingdom must flee from the wrath to come.

What terrible language the Lord Jesus uses in these parables to depict the fate of the wicked!

A furnace of fire! Wailing and gnashing of teeth! Some are quick to say these are just figures of speech, so they are not to be taken literally. Yet the question remains: What kind of fate is it that requires such terrible figures to convey it? It must be a dreadful thing indeed.

Contrast this with what the Lord Jesus had to say about the fate of the righteous, that is, they 'will shine forth as the sun in the kingdom of their Father' (v. 43).

THINK ABOUT IT

The furnace, constructed of brick or stone, was used to 'smelt ore, melt metal for casting, heat metal for forging, fire pottery or bricks, and to make lime'. The Bible uses the word to convey experiences of terrible suffering (Deuteronomy 4:20; 1 Kings 8:51; Isaiah 48:10; Jeremiah 11:4). It was, therefore, a fitting symbol for the judgement that awaits the wicked.[2]

REMEMBER THIS

Just as hell is indescribably horrendous, so heaven is indescribably glorious. And make no mistake about it, Jesus Christ makes the difference between hell and heaven. Only those who repent of their sins and receive him as their king are accepted into his kingdom, and only those who are accepted into his kingdom are spared from the fate of the wicked.

DISCUSS IT

1. Read Ephesians 6:10-20. Did the apostle Paul believe in Satan? What does he teach about resisting Satan?

2. What is Satan's final destiny? Read Revelation 20:7-10.

3. Is the church to ignore evil in its midst? Read 1 Corinthians 5.

CHAPTER FOURTEEN

COMFORT FOR THOSE WHO ARE LONELY

LOOK IT UP

'At my first defence no one stood with me... But the Lord stood with me and strengthened me...'
(2 Timothy 4:16-17).

Suggested reading: Isaiah 41:8-10

INTRODUCTION

A truth capsule

'A gust of loneliness can sometimes chill a faithful heart.'[1]

(E. M. Blaiklock)

Some points to ponder

'No one'

From a prison in Rome, the apostle Paul wrote his second letter to Timothy. The apostle himself was in the midst of very difficult and trying circumstances, but he was primarily concerned about Timothy and his situation.

As he draws his letter to a conclusion, Paul makes reference to some of the things he had faced in Rome. He mentions the harm that he had suffered from Alexander the coppersmith (2 Timothy 4:14). Some commentators think that this man had been instrumental in having Paul arrested. Others think he may have served as the leading witness against Paul in court.[2]

While the harm done by Alexander had been very painful for Paul, we gain the distinct impression that he felt even more pain over being abandoned by those he expected to stand with him. Here are his sad words: 'At my first defence no one stood with me, but all forsook me' (v. 16).

THINK ABOUT IT

The apostle Paul was not alone in his loneliness. Job expressed loneliness in these words:

'He has removed my brothers far from me,
And my acquaintances are completely estranged from me.
My relatives have failed,
And my close friends have forgotten me.
Those who dwell in my house, and my maidservants,
Count me as a stranger;
I am an alien in their sight.
I call my servant, but he gives no answer;
I beg him with my mouth.
My breath is offensive to my wife,
And I am repulsive to the children of my own body.
Even young children despise me;

I arise, and they speak against me.
All my close friends abhor me,
And those whom I love have turned
against me'

(Job 19:13-19).

David, the wonderful psalmist of Israel, expressed his loneliness in these words:

I am like a pelican of the wilderness;
I am like an owl of the desert.
I lie awake,
And am like a sparrow alone on the
housetop

(Psalm 102:6-7).

Geoffrey Wilson writes: 'All the Christians in Rome deserted him in his hour of need.'³

The apostle's generous and charitable spirit is displayed in his next phrase: 'May it not be charged against them' (v. 16). The fact that Paul was so very ready to forgive should not be taken to mean that the abandonment was not very distressing to him. Christians do not forgive only when the hurt has been slight but also when it is very deep.

Paul's words resonate with multitudes of believers today, who find themselves in the midst of very demanding circumstances. They feel that they could find strength to face their situation if only they had someone who understood and cared, but it appears as if they are left to fend for themselves. They are alone, and 'No one stands with me' is their plaintive cry.

Loneliness is not the same as solitude. One can be lonely in the midst of a crowd. The sick and dying can feel lonely with medical personnel swarming all around. The bereaved can feel lonely even with family members hovering near. The overworked can feel lonely with co-workers milling about. The backslider can feel lonely in a packed church service. The one who stands for the truth can feel lonely even though he is affiliated with a large denomination.

What is that believer who feels abandoned and forsaken to do? He must do as Paul did; he must find company and comfort in the Lord.

THINK ABOUT IT

Warren Wiersbe writes: 'Loneliness is being all by yourself even when you're surrounded by people. Loneliness is a feeling of isolation even in the midst of a crowd. You feel unwanted. You feel unneeded. You feel as though there's nothing to live for. You feel as though nobody really cares anymore. That's loneliness. Loneliness eats away at the inner person. It saps you of strength. It robs you of hope. Loneliness, as it were, puts a wall around you no matter how free you may be.'[4]

'But the Lord'

Paul was abandoned by friends and fellow-believers while he was in the crucible of difficulty. He could have let this experience drive him into self-pity and despair, but he refused to do so. He turned instead to his never-failing friend, the Lord Jesus Christ. This enabled him to write: 'But the Lord stood with me and strengthened me' (v. 17).

The Lord always stands with his people. He stands with them when their suffering is great. He stands with them when their faith is small. He stands with them when no one else will.

Many Christians do not hesitate to say that the most precious promise in times of adversity is the Lord's promise to be with his people (Isaiah 43:2, 5; Matthew 28:20; Hebrews 13:5). The promise of his presence has often been used by God's people to comfort each other. When another Christian is facing difficulty and hardship, we almost instinctively ask the Lord to be 'with' them, and we might even say to them, 'The Lord is with you.'

Have you ever wondered how this helps? How is the Lord with his people in their trials and tribulations? What is there about his presence that brings comfort to them?

We can answer such questions by saying the Lord is with us in various ways.

- He is with us as a *sympathizer*. He understands and cares. Not one ache of our hearts is unimportant to him (Hebrews 4:14-16; 1 Peter 5:6-7).

- He is with us as a *sustainer*. He is actually there to give us strength, grace and wisdom — even when it seems that we are completely without these things (2 Corinthians 12:9; Philippians 4:13).

- He is with us as a wise *strategist*. Everything he allows to come our way is for our good and for his glory (Romans 8:28).

- He is with us as a *preserver*. Nothing, absolutely nothing, can ever destroy our relationship with him. We are more than conquerors through him (Psalm 121:7-8; Romans 8:37).

- He is with us as a *deliverer*. In his own time and way, he will bring us through our difficulties. And, of course, the greatest deliverance of all is when he finally takes us home to himself, where nothing harmful or hurtful will ever be able to touch us again (2 Timothy 4:18).

With the confidence that the Lord is with us in all these ways, God's people can triumphantly say with the psalmist:

When my father and my mother forsake me,
Then the LORD will take care of me

(Psalm 27:10).

REMEMBER THIS

All of this raises a very important and vital question, namely, how do we know the Lord is with us? The cross of Christ proves for ever how God feels about his people. Take a long and hard look at it. See the blood streaming down. See that disfigured face. Hear the voices of mockery, ridicule and scorn. See the sun hiding her face and darkness gathering all around. Hear that piercing cry: 'My God, my God, why have you forsaken me?', and understand as you hear it that Jesus Christ was there bearing your sin and the wrath it deserved.

Look long enough at Calvary's cross until this divine logic is drilled for ever into your heart — if God was willing to go to that extent to make us his children, we need never question that he will be with us. Being with us is less than what he has done for us on the cross. If he did that for us, we should never doubt that he will do lesser things.

QUESTIONS FOR DISCUSSION

1. Read Numbers 11:10-15. What type of loneliness was Moses facing at this time?

2. Read 1 Kings 19. What type of loneliness was Elijah facing?

3. Think about Paul's prayer that those who had forsaken him should not be charged with it. Read Acts 7:54-60. Who prayed the same prayer in these verses? Who was present on this occasion? (v. 58). What name would he later take? (13:9).

CHAPTER FIFTEEN

COMFORT FOR THOSE WHO ARE SPIRITUALLY DEPRESSED

LOOK IT UP

O God, you are my God;
Early will I seek you;
My soul thirsts for you;
My flesh longs for you
In a dry and thirsty land
Where there is no water.
So I have looked for you
in the sanctuary,
To see your power and
your glory
(Psalm 63:1-2).

Suggested reading: Psalms 42 & 43

A truth capsule

INTRODUCTION

We do not have to actually go into a barren region to have a wilderness experience. There is a sense in which all of the Christian life in this world can be called a wilderness experience. We Christians are citizens of heaven (Philippians 3:20), and while we are in this world we are separated from our true home and faced with hardships and dangers.

As we walk through this wilderness world, we often find ourselves encountering circumstances and difficulties that make it seem even more barren and God even more distant. We fall into sinful living. We are beset by trials and afflictions. We feel coldness in our hearts towards the Lord, and we find his work to be tiresome and monotonous. When we experience such things we are in something of a spiritual wilderness.

There are times in which the church as a whole seems to go through such a spiritual wilderness, times in which her zeal for the Lord flags, and she is infiltrated by worldly thinking and doing.

THINK ABOUT IT

David wrote this psalm while in the wilderness. The wilderness was a barren, desolate place where he was deprived of the comforts of home and exposed to bad weather and hostile enemies.

These things were in and of themselves enough to make the wilderness a very troubling and trying experience. David found it to be even more so for another reason. While in the wilderness he was away from the sanctuary of the Lord (v. 2).

There are those who tell us that the child of God should never go through a spiritual wilderness, that he should never feel barren and desolate spiritually. But most of us know that it is inevitable for us to have such times. Even though David was one of God's most favoured and blessed, he was not exempt from the wilderness experience he describes in this psalm.

Some points to ponder

The question is not whether we as God's people will have to go through wilderness experiences, but rather how to face them. It is at this point that David's psalm offers tremendous help.

Occupied with God

It first shows us that David occupied himself with God and not with the wilderness. How easy it would have been for David to be preoccupied with his wilderness experience! The heading of this psalm tells us that it was written when David was in the wilderness of Judah. Why was he there? King Saul was seeking his life! (1 Samuel 22).

What a difficult time this was for David! Although he had been anointed by the prophet Samuel to be Saul's successor, he appeared to be nowhere near coming to the throne. And even though he, David, had been nothing to the king except a loyal and devoted subject, he was a fugitive. He had gone into battle on behalf of Saul and Israel and defeated the giant Goliath. He had played soothing music to ease the anguish of the troubled and tormented Saul. But Saul, feeling no gratitude for these things, was filled with bitter envy and murderous rage towards David.

David certainly had moments when he allowed the difficulty of his situation to occupy

EXPLANATION

him (1 Samuel 27:1), but this was the exception rather than the rule. For the most part, he responded to his difficulties and burdens by occupying himself with God.

Psalm 63 is an example of this. David could have asked why these things were happening to him. He could have allowed himself to become bitter towards God. He could have begun to doubt whether the promises of God would be fulfilled. Instead he begins this psalm by crying out:

> O God, you are my God:
> Early will I seek you:
> My soul thirsts for you:
> My flesh longs for you
> In a dry and thirsty land...

It is not enough for us merely to observe that David occupied himself with God. He reminded himself of particular details about God, namely, that he, God, had in grace entered into a covenant relationship with his people. It was on this basis and this basis alone that David was able to call him 'my God'.

David also reminded himself of the lovingkindness of God, that is, those kind acts of God that flowed from a heart of love (v. 3). He recalled how God had been his help in the past (v. 7).

On the basis of God's previous kindness to him, David knew he had nothing to fear. The same God who had tenderly cared for him in the past could be counted on to continue to do the same.

With this psalm David teaches us one of the most important and vital lessons we can ever learn: the more occupied we are with God and his heart of love for his children, the more bearable our trials and difficulties will be.

THINK ABOUT IT

David says the love of God is better than life itself. James Montgomery Boice explains: 'The word he uses is *hesed*, which is often translated "lovingkindness" or "covenant-love". It stresses the faithful continuance of God's love. God's love is steady and unchangeable, which is why it is better than even the best thing in life, which is life itself. Life itself can be lost, even though we value it and try to protect it at all costs. However, the covenant-love of God can never be lost.'[1]

Resolved to pursue God

This psalm also shows us that David coped with his wilderness experience by resolving to pursue God vigorously.

This is a psalm of solemn determination. David resolved to seek the Lord (v. 1), to bless the Lord (v. 4), and to lift up his hands, which was synonymous with prayer (v. 4, see also Psalm

38:2). He was also determined to praise the Lord with 'joyful lips' (v. 5), to meditate on the Lord during the night (v. 6) and to rejoice in the Lord's protective care of him (v. 7).

All of this takes us a step further and shows us how to go about occupying ourselves with God. It requires diligent and determined effort.

This brings us face to face with a gigantic failure in the lives of many Christians: desiring God's presence and his help in times of trial and difficulty without ever giving ourselves to a determined and devoted pursuit of God. We often want what God can give us rather than God himself.

Persuaded of glory in the future

Finally, this psalm shows us that David was able to cope with his wilderness because he was persuaded that he could see the glory and power of God even at such barren times. He writes:

So I have looked for you in the sanctuary,
To see your power and your glory

(v. 2).

Some take those words to mean that David was expressing his fervent hope that he would soon be delivered from his wilderness experience and once again be able to join in public worship. There can be no doubt that this was indeed the desire of David's heart.

But other scholars suggest that David was saying something quite different. They understand David to be addressing God in this way: 'I desire to see your glory and your power in the wilderness as I have seen it in the sanctuary.'

If this view is correct, David was reminding himself that God was not limited to the tabernacle. He certainly felt anguish over being separated from public worship, even as every child of God should feel a keen sense of loss when he is not able to be in the house of the Lord. But David knew the Lord could reveal himself right there in the wilderness. How wilderness living is transformed when one is able to see the glory and power of the Lord!

Perhaps the greatest question facing Christians today is whether we believe we can see the glory and power of the Lord in the wilderness. Do we as individuals believe that the Lord can come to us in the midst of our difficulties and make his presence known to us? Do we believe the Lord can come to his entire church and bring renewal and power? Do we believe in revival for the church? Revival is that time when God comes to his church in the midst of the wilderness and pours out his blessings upon her, and those times when he reveals his glory and power to her.

REMEMBER THIS

The church these days seems to spend much of her time lamenting the wilderness. There is so very much to lament! The devil and his forces seem so very strong and we seem so very weak.

There is, however, nothing to be gained from merely repeating the evils of the times. Instead of merely lamenting the wilderness, let us remind ourselves of those glorious periods in history when the Lord made his glory known to his church. Let us devote our lives to seeking the Lord, saying with David:

My soul thirsts for you:
My flesh longs for you
In a dry and thirsty land
Where there is no water

(v. 1).

QUESTIONS FOR DISCUSSION

1. Read Psalm 84 for another example of David's longing to be engaged in public worship. Was his longing intense and fervent? What blessings did he expect to receive?

DISCUSS IT

2. Read 1 Chronicles 20 for another example of someone who occupied himself with God in the midst of serious trouble. Who was this man? What was the situation?

3. Read Philippians 1 for yet another example of a believer focusing on the Lord in the midst of difficulties. Here the imprisoned apostle Paul rejoices in God. What reasons does he give for doing so?

CHAPTER SIXTEEN

COMFORT FOR THOSE WHO DESPAIR OVER THE CAUSE OF GOD

LOOK IT UP

Your eyes will see the King in his beauty;
They will see the land that is very far off...
Look upon Zion, the city of our appointed feasts;
Your eyes will see Jerusalem, a quiet home,
A tabernacle that will not be taken down;
Not one of its stakes will ever be removed,
Nor will any of its cords be broken
(Isaiah 33:17, 20).

Suggested reading: Psalm 2; 90:13-17

INTRODUCTION

A truth capsule

It was a terribly grim and dreary time in the life of the kingdom of Judah. The Assyrians, under their king, Sennacherib, had laid siege to the city of Jerusalem. Other cities had fallen to the dreaded Assyrians, and now here they were surrounding the city of Jerusalem. All access to neighbouring towns and villages was cut off, and turbulence reigned inside Jerusalem. There was no domestic tranquillity. There were no happy conversations. The people were terrified.

To make things worse, the people of Judah noticed that King Hezekiah had shed his royal robe to don the garb of someone in mourning and lamenting. The people of the city were devastated to see their king dressed in sackcloth.

THINK ABOUT IT

Sackcloth was coarse, black cloth usually made of goats' hair. It was worn to depict grief and mourning for the dead, mourning for a personal or national disaster, repentance for one's sins or desire for deliverance. It was usually worn next to the skin.[1]

Some points to ponder

Isaiah's message to Judah

The prophet Isaiah stepped into this situation with a happy message. There were two points to this message. First, he spoke of things the people of Jerusalem would see; then he spoke of things those same people would not see.

1. Things the people would see

Isaiah assured the people that the Assyrian siege would not continue. The land that now seemed to them to be so far away, their neighbouring towns, would be seen again. Furthermore, he promised that they would again see quiet in Jerusalem. It was anything but quiet now, but calm would return. It would again be a peaceful home.

Because the Assyrians seemed so very strong, many inhabitants of Jerusalem undoubtedly thought they would never again see Hezekiah dressed in his royal

robe. But Isaiah promised his hearers that their king would not continue to wear sackcloth. They would again see the king in his beauty.

2. Things they would not see

Isaiah says:

> 'Where is the scribe?
> Where is he who weighs?
> Where is he who counts the towers?'
>
> (v. 18).

These are all references to officials of the Assyrian army. Isaiah was promising that a day would come when these officials would be seen no more.

THINK ABOUT IT

The word 'scribe' refers to one who counts or numbers and may refer to a secretary who had the responsibility of reviewing and numbering the army. The 'weigher' may refer to the treasurer who was responsible for overseeing the tribute received and for paying the army. The tower-counter probably indicates the one who had the responsibility of estimating the defensive strength of the enemy.[2]

The prophet then adds these words:

You will not see a fierce people,
A people of obscure speech, beyond perception,
Of a stammering tongue that you cannot understand
(v. 19).

The Assyrians would not be seen again. The people
of Jerusalem had been terrified of them. Isaiah essentially says, 'You have been scared to death of these
Assyrians. You have been scared because of their fierce
looks. You have been scared because you have heard
them speak in a language you did not understand. But
you are not going to see them any more, and you are
not going to hear them.'

Isaiah's message must have sounded like the message of a fool when he first delivered it. Perhaps some
of the people chided him. Perhaps some said, 'Isaiah,
you have taken leave of your senses. Don't you know
what these Assyrians have done? Other cities were
hoping for the very same things that you have talked
about, but their hopes were not fulfilled. Instead they
continued to see the things you have said we will not
see. They continued to see the military officials and
the fierce look in the eyes of the soldiers. Why should
we be any different from those who have already fallen
to the Assyrians?'

But there was a triumphant certainty in Isaiah's
words. He said, 'Your eyes will see the King in his
beauty.' And it was delivered with utmost conviction.

All that Isaiah prophesied came true. The Lord suddenly struck the army of the Assyrians with some sort of pestilence or plague, and after 185,000 of them died, Sennacherib packed his bags and went home (2 Kings 19:35-36).

Isaiah's message to us

Isaiah's message contains great comfort and encouragement for us. There is a very real sense in which every Christian can take Isaiah's words as his own and with utmost conviction say to his fellow-Christian, 'Your eyes will see the King in his beauty' (v. 17).

These words lead us to ponder two truths.

1. In Christ Christians have a beautiful King

Here is something, Christian, of the beauty of Christ your King. It is the beauty of God himself; it is the beauty of eternality; it is the beauty of sovereignty; it is the beauty of heavenly splendour; it is the beauty of holiness; it is the beauty of abundant mercy; it is the beauty of truth; it is the beauty of perfect faithfulness; it is the beauty of uncompromised justice.

We do not have the line to plumb this depth. We can only join the apostle Paul in marvelling that in Christ all fulness dwells (Colossians 1:19).

EXPLANATION

2. The beauty of Christ our King is not always visible

Jesus' public ministry. Think about the earthly life and
ministry of our Lord. While he was here upon the earth,
he was still King. He did not lose any of his deity. He
was still King; but his kingship was cloaked while he
was here.

Let us look back to Bethlehem's stable. There the
Lord Jesus is lying in that manger in swaddling clothes,
and I ask: 'Does he appear to be the King of kings and
the Lord of lords?'

Yes, he was King even while he was lying in that
crude stable, but his kingship was not visible. Of course,
there were some trappings of it. The angels announced
his birth to the shepherds. But generally speaking, his
kingship was hidden.

Follow him now to Nazareth and to the carpenter's
shop of Joseph. He appears there to be anything but a
king. Then follow him into his public ministry. On
occasions he revealed something of his majesty and
glory. On the Mount of Transfiguration he pulled back,
as it were, the robe of his humanity so his underlying
glory could be seen. But that was an exception, and it
was a revelation to only three disciples. For the most
part the kingship of Christ was veiled during his earthly
ministry. It was hidden. It was not obvious.

The Lord Jesus himself said that the birds had their
nests and the foxes their holes (Matthew 8:20), but he
would have nowhere to lay his head. If you and I could
go back in time and ask the multitudes who followed

EXPLANATION

Jesus if he was the King of kings, they would have laughed at the suggestion. They would have pointed to his poverty, to the handful of disciples around him and to the nature of those common, ordinary men, and they would have said, 'Whatever else he may be, he is not a king, let alone the King of kings.'

Follow him further and you find him paraded and prodded through the streets of Jerusalem and taken to the hill of Golgotha where he is nailed to a cross. That cross is lifted and he is suspended between heaven and earth. Those who passed by and saw him there would never have guessed that Jesus was King of kings and Lord of lords. Because there on that cross he was dying the most ignominious death a man could die.

After he died they laid his body in a borrowed tomb. Perhaps someone said, 'That seals it. He did not have a tomb of his own. How could he have been a king?'

The church. It is not only a matter of looking at the life and death of Jesus, it is also a matter of looking at the church today. She is often so very weak and pathetic. Most churches cannot muster half their members for any one service. And many who do attend carry cold hearts. Many churches are torn by dissension and resentment. In the midst of it all, her testimony is that she serves the Lord Jesus who is King of kings. And the surrounding world is quick to observe and to pronounce that the church's testimony is not true.

The situation is such that many Christians, weary of trying to be faithful to the Lord in a sceptical and hostile world, may very well be wondering if they will ever see the King in his beauty. There is good news for all heavy-hearted Christians, for all saints who are buffeted by doubt. The Lord Jesus Christ will come again. The dead in Christ will be raised from their graves and rejoined to their souls, which went to be with the Lord when they died. Those who are alive and remain shall be caught up to meet the Lord in the air (1 Thessalonians 4:13-18). And on that glorious day every single child of God will see the King in his beauty. All doubts will be vanished for ever; all questions removed for ever.

Face to face I shall behold Him,
Far beyond the starry skies;
Face to face in all His glory,
I shall see Him by and by![3]

(Carrie E. Breck)

On that day we shall certainly be dazzled by the sovereignty, the glory and the splendour of the Lord Jesus Christ. But the thing that will be most precious to us will be the sight of him in our humanity. Yes, when he took our humanity, he did it for ever. He is in that humanity now. It is, of course, a changed humanity, but it is still humanity. When he comes, he will be in that humanity.

Crown Him the Lord of love;
Behold His hands and side,
Those wounds, yet visible above,
In beauty glorified...

(Matthew Bridges 1800-94
and Godfrey Thring 1823-1903).

When we see him in that humanity and note those wounds, we will be amazed that the beautiful King from eternity past would have gone to such lengths to redeem his people.

REMEMBER THIS

REMEMBER THIS

When the Lord Jesus comes for his people, it will be for the purpose of finally ushering them into the New Jerusalem. That city will be the saints' 'quiet home'. Nothing will ever trouble them there. And they will dwell there for ever. It will indeed be the tabernacle that will not be 'taken down', and none of its stakes will 'ever be removed' (Isaiah 33:20).

The Assyrians are still around today, and Sennacherib is here as well. They go by different names, but they still disturb the people of God with their scepticism and their doubts. We need not fear them. All God's people will see the King in his beauty and they will enter the quiet habitation he has prepared for them. What glory awaits the children of God!

QUESTIONS FOR DISCUSSION

1. *Read Psalm 27:4; 96:6. Where did the psalmist expect to see the beauty of the Lord?*

2. *Read Psalm 45 as a picture of Christ receiving his bride. Does the Lord Jesus see beauty in his people? Read Isaiah 61:10. What makes Christ's people beautiful to him?*

3. *Read Revelation 5 for a description of that time when Christ's beauty will be apparent to all. What song will the redeemed sing at that time?*

CHAPTER SEVENTEEN

COMFORT FOR BATTERED SAINTS

LOOK IT UP

'And the Lord said, "Simon, Simon! Indeed, Satan has asked for you, that he may sift you as wheat. But I have prayed for you that your faith should not fail; and when you have returned to me, strengthen your brethren"'
(Luke 22:31-32).

Suggested reading: John 17:20-26

A truth capsule

INTRODUCTION

As we look at the Lord's words, we have no trouble seeing that he was emphasizing two truths: the reality of Satan's sifting and the reality of his own tender care for Simon.

These realities are as much in place today as they were then. Satan is still in the sifting business, and the Lord Jesus still cares for his people. These are not, however, equal realities. Christ's care is far greater than Satan's sieve.

Some points to ponder

It was the night before the Lord Jesus Christ was crucified. What an eventful night it was! The Lord Jesus met with his disciples in the Upper Room where he washed their feet and instituted the Lord's Supper. There also the disciples had once again argued about which of them was the greatest in the kingdom.

Against that backdrop the Lord Jesus turned to speak to Simon some very solemn and searching words. We know that these words were special because the Lord Jesus prefaced them with, 'Simon, Simon', the repetition indicating how the Lord wished to emphasize them.

THINK ABOUT IT

A sieve was an instrument that farmers used to separate chaff from wheat. A farmer would pour his wheat into the sieve, take it into his hands and shake it from side to side. As he did this, the wheat would settle to the bottom and fall through the tiny holes in the base. What was left in the sieve was coarse material that would be removed and destroyed.

When the farmer shook the sieve, however, the wheat itself would be thrown from side to side. It would be battered.

Two realities

1. Satan's sieve

While the Lord spoke specifically to Simon, he had all his disciples in mind. The first 'you' in these verses is plural. The second 'you' is singular and indicates that the Lord was at that point focusing exclusively on Simon.

On this particular night all the disciples of Jesus were about to experience a heart-wrenching time. They were about to experience the battering of Satan. He had them in his sieve and he was about to shake them from side to side.

Satan's purpose in shaking and battering the disciples was to knock their faith right out of them. He wanted to show them to be chaff instead of wheat. At the end of the process, his desire was to be able to say something like this to the Lord: 'Here are these disciples whom you have chosen and whom you are planning to elevate to such high positions in the church. Let me tell you, they are more chaff than wheat, and I will prove it by shaking them in my sieve.'

We might say Satan had asked permission to do with the disciples as he had done long before with Job. On that occasion he, Satan, had come to God to suggest that Job was chaff instead of wheat (Job 1:6-12; 2:1-7). The Lord gave Satan permission to put Job in his sieve. The Lord knew he was wheat and that Satan's shaking would only confirm it.

Satan did as he was permitted to do. He put Job in his sieve, and he shook. Oh, how he shook Job! Job lost his family, his health and his possessions. As we read the account, we might very well find ourselves thinking that Satan had indeed succeeded. It often appears that Job's faith is hanging by a mere thread and that thread is doomed to snap. But when the book ends, Job emerges from Satan's sieve as wheat.

The Lord's warning to Simon speaks powerfully to us. Satan still wants to knock the faith out of God's people, and he has all kinds of ways of battering us. He may stir various ones to deride and ridicule our faith. He may point us to the failure of a believer whom we have prized and respected. He may point us to elite unbelievers, the rich, the powerful, the popular, and say, 'You see, these people do not believe in your Christianity. You are out of step.' He will most certainly point us to our own sins, and on that basis tell us we are not true children of God.

Simon Peter was only hours away from denying the Lord Jesus Christ. When Simon later played out those denials, he 'wept bitterly' (Luke 22:62). We can well imagine Simon saying to himself, 'Satan did it! He knocked the faith right out of me. He proved that I am chaff and not wheat. If I were wheat, I would not have denied my Lord.'

Satan has a long memory, and when it comes to sin, he makes sure the believer's memory is also long. Maybe that sin is twenty years old, but Satan still resurrects it and says, 'You see, you are not wheat. You're chaff, and you're not even good chaff at that. You're the worst kind of chaff there is.'

Do we have anything to say to those believers who are so keenly aware of being battered and shaken by

Satan? Indeed we do. We can tell them that Satan's battering, no matter how harsh it may seem, will not finally be effective. Satan cannot ultimately destroy the faith of any believer in Christ. Why is this so? The answer is in the second reality of our text.

2. The Saviour's care

EXPLANATION

How we should rejoice that the Lord Jesus did not rely on Simon for the outcome of Simon's faith! The Lord took responsibility for that upon himself.

We have a tendency to think that faith is ours, that we must create and sustain it. The truth of the matter is that faith is Christ's. He is the giver of it, and he is the sustainer of it. The author of Hebrews calls him 'the author and finisher of our faith' (Hebrews 12:2).

While Satan can attack faith and lessen, diminish and reduce it, he can never destroy it. The Lord Jesus himself said, 'My sheep hear my voice, and I know them, and they follow me. And I give them eternal life, and they shall never perish; neither shall anyone snatch them out of my hand. My Father, who has given them to me, is greater than all; and no one is able to snatch them out of my Father's hand' (John 10:27-29).

The only way Satan could destroy true faith is if he were stronger than the Lord Jesus Christ.

He is not. How do we know Christ is stronger than
Satan? Look to that empty grave outside Jerusalem. It
testifies that Jesus Christ has authority over all. He has
authority over death, hell, the grave and all the tools
and devices of Satan.

One way that Jesus Christ sustains the faith of his
people is by praying for them. On this occasion, the
Lord Jesus did not say to Simon, 'You are going to be
shaken by Satan. You had better pray for yourself.'

There is certainly nothing wrong with anyone praying for himself when he is battered by Satan, but many
saints in Satan's sieve have found themselves so beaten
and bruised that they could not pray. All they could do
was weep.

Neither did the Lord Jesus tell Simon to ask the other
disciples to pray for him. There would not have been
anything wrong with that, but their prayers could not
begin to compare with the prayers of the Lord Jesus,
and the Lord here assures Simon that he would be
praying for him. The Lord had already prayed for Simon
on that night, and he would pray for him yet again in
the Garden of Gethsemane. Indeed, the Bible also tells
us that Jesus prayed that same night for all his disciples, even his future disciples (John 17:6, 9, 20).

After he arose from the grave, he ascended to the
Father in heaven. He is even now at the right hand of
God, where he prays for his people, making interces-
sion on their behalf (Hebrews 7:25).

What consolation there is in knowing the Saviour
prays for his people! His praying is specific. He knows

EXPLANATION

each of his people and each burden and sorrow they bear. His praying is constant. While his people often fail in their praying, he never fails in his. His praying is effective. He will never lose one of his people. He will bring each one of his children home; not one will be missing. When we finally come into his presence, we will not say we are there by virtue of our own wisdom to outwit Satan or our own power to defeat him. We will rather confess triumphantly that we are there because the Lord Jesus who gave us faith sustained it.

We can, therefore, join John Newton in singing:

Through many dangers, toils, and snares,
I have already come;
'Tis grace hath brought me safe thus far,
And grace will lead me home.[1]

THINK ABOUT IT

After a turbulent and rebellious youth when he was engaged in slave trade, John Newton was converted to Christ after surviving a violent storm in the North Atlantic. He then spent a long life as a faithful minister of the gospel, before his death in 1807. The following words were inscribed on his tombstone:

John Newton,
Clerk,
Once an infidel and libertine,
A servant of slaves in Africa,
Was
By the rich mercy of our Lord and Saviour
Jesus Christ,
Preserved, restored, pardoned,
And appointed to preach the faith
He had long laboured to destroy.[2]

One piercing question

Most of us find it quite impossible to read the Lord's words to Simon Peter without asking this question: 'Why would the Lord allow his people to be put in Satan's sieve?' He certainly does not have to do so as he is greater than Satan.

We may rest assured that we will never be able to answer that question to our complete satisfaction, but we can consider at least two reasons while we wait for the final answer.

The first is that the Lord strengthens the faith of his people by putting them in Satan's sieve. Faith is like gold. As gold is refined by fire, so faith is refined by difficulties. It is made stronger and better by hardship.

The other reason is conveyed to us by these words the Lord Jesus spoke to Simon Peter: 'When you have returned to me, strengthen your brethren' (v. 32).

EXPLANATION

The Lord allowed Simon to be battered by Satan so that he would come out of that experience stronger and wiser. And as that stronger, wiser Christian he would, through his writings, prove to be a source of unspeakable blessing to every generation of believers. One wonders whether this great apostle would have been able to write the following words with clarity and conviction had he not been battered in Satan's sieve:

Therefore humble yourselves under the mighty hand of God, that he may exalt you in due time, casting all your cares upon him, for he cares for you. Be sober, be vigilant; because your adversary the devil walks about like a roaring lion, seeking whom he may devour. Resist him, steadfast in the faith, knowing that the same sufferings are experienced by your brotherhood in the world. But may the God of all grace, who called us to his eternal glory by Christ Jesus, after you have suffered a while, perfect, establish, strengthen, and settle you. To him be the glory and the dominion for ever and ever. Amen' (1 Peter 5:6-11).

May all who find themselves in Satan's sieve learn from Peter's words. The sieve will never knock the faith out of us, but in God's good purpose, when we emerge we can help those who are still there.

REMEMBER THIS

While the Lord Jesus Christ has a tender concern for his feeble people, he himself was not feeble in his redeeming work. How very thankful we should be for his unswerving loyalty to God the Father and to his steadfast determination to carry out his mission. Speaking of his death on the cross, the Lord said, '…for this purpose I came to this hour' (John 12:27). When the time came for him to go to Jerusalem to die on the cross, he 'steadfastly set his face' (Luke 9:51). And immediately before he died, he cried out: 'It is finished!' (John 19:30).

QUESTIONS FOR DISCUSSION

1. *In what ways can we show the tenderness of Christ to fellow believers who are bruised? Read Romans 12:15; Galatians 6:1-2; James 4:11-12; 5:13-18.*

2. *Read Romans 8:29-39. What answer does Paul expect his readers to give to his questions in verses 31-35? Was Paul convinced that the faith of God's elect will never be lost?*

3. *Read John 21. How did Jesus show tenderness to Simon Peter in this chapter?*

CHAPTER EIGHTEEN

COMFORT FOR
THE CARERS

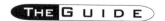
LOOK IT UP

BIBLE REFERENCE

'For God is not unjust to forget your work and labour of love which you have shown towards his name, in that you have ministered to the saints, and do minister' (Hebrews 6:10).

'But do not forget to do good and to share, for with such sacrifices God is well pleased' (Hebrews 13:16).

'And God is able to make all grace abound towards you, that you, always having all sufficiency in all things, may have an abundance for every good work... For the administration of this service not only supplies the needs of the saints, but also is abounding through many thanksgivings to God, while, through the proof of this ministry, they glorify God for the obedience of your confession to the gospel of Christ, and for your liberal sharing with them...' (2 Corinthians 9:8, 12-13).

Suggested reading: John 13:1-17

A truth capsule

While all Christians are called to care for others, some are called to care in ways that are so very demanding and taxing that they often feel as if their strength is depleted and can never be replenished. Those who provide care for the mentally ill, the aged and the terminally ill are some examples. Where can such carers find help to go on with their tasks? The above verses provide care for the carers.

Some points to ponder

We know the apostle Paul wrote the letter of 2 Corinthians. Many think he also wrote the letter to the Hebrews, but we cannot say this with any degree of certainty. We can, however, be certain about the purpose behind these verses. The verses from 2 Corinthians 9 are part of the appeal Paul was making for the believers in Corinth to give generously to their fellow believers in Jerusalem.

The verses from Hebrews were written to encourage believers in Christ to maintain good works as 'things that accompany salvation' (6:9). These good works certainly include ministry to the needs of fellow believers (6:10). In dealing with their separate concerns, these authors uncover some encouraging truths for carers.

The Christian's provision of care is to God

The author of Hebrews refers to the 'work and labour of love' (Hebrews 6:10) that his readers had been manifesting. Carers would have no difficulty writing a commentary on the labour that is involved in giving care. The hours are long and the stress can be intense. How the labour is transformed by the author's next phrase — 'which you have shown towards his name'!

With these words the writer was merely repeating the truth originally taught by the Lord Jesus himself: 'Then the righteous will answer him saying, "Lord, when did we see you hungry and feed you, or thirsty and give you drink? When did we see you a stranger and take you in, or naked and clothe you? Or when did we see you sick, or in prison, and come to you?" And the King will answer and say to them, "Assuredly, I say to you, inasmuch as you did it to one of the least of these my brethren, you did it to me"' (Matthew 25:37-40).

If we keep our eyes only on the situation with which we are dealing, we will usually find plenty of reason for discouragement. But if we see our ministry as to the Lord, the labour becomes a delight. It then becomes our way of expressing love and gratitude to the one who so graciously gave of himself to save us from condemnation.

God will not forget

The author provides another encouraging truth with these words: 'For God is not unjust to forget your work and labour of love… ' (Hebrews 6:10).

Those to whom carers minister may be in such a condition that they are not even aware of the sacrificial nature of the service being rendered to them. Or they may recuperate and largely forget what was done on their behalf. But God does not forget. His nature does not allow him to forget. Geoffrey Wilson writes: 'Since God is not unrighteous he cannot fail to reward the service which a reverence for his name inspired...'[1]

This truth caused John Trapp to reflect on Genesis 40:1-23 and 41:50-51, and to observe: 'The butler may forget Joseph, and Joseph forget his father's house; but forgetfulness befalls not God, to whom all things are present...'[2]

God is well pleased

As the author of Hebrews wraps up his epistle, he once again encourages his readers 'to do good and to share' (Hebrews 13:16). We might say that he encourages them to be carers. And he offers them this marvellous incentive for doing so: God is delighted with them. Every act of service rendered in the name of the Lord and for his glory is to him like the fragrant aroma of a sacrifice (Genesis 8:21).

In his letter to the Philippians, the apostle Paul mentions the ministry he had received from Epaphroditus. He characterizes this ministry as 'a sweet-smelling aroma, an acceptable sacrifice, well pleasing to God' (Philippians 4:18).

These days many seem to have the idea that God is hard to please. The problem is not that God is so hard to please, but rather that we find it so hard to do the things that please him.

THINK ABOUT IT

THINK ABOUT IT

Animal sacrifice was instituted by God himself in the Garden of Eden after Adam and Eve sinned (Genesis 3:21). The first time a sacrifice was described as providing a fragrant aroma for God was that of Noah after he left the ark (Genesis 8:20-22). The implication of the phrase 'fragrant aroma' or 'soothing aroma' is that the sacrifice propitiated the wrath of God against human sin. There was, of course, no way for an animal sacrifice to actually deal with human sin, but they could and did serve as types or pictures of Jesus voluntarily sacrificing himself on behalf of sinners. That sacrifice truly propitiated or appeased God (Romans 3:25; 1 John 2:2).

God can make grace abound

We find a further encouraging truth in Paul's words to the Corinthians: 'And God is able to make all grace abound towards you, that you, always having all sufficiency in all things, may have an abundance for every good work...' (2 Corinthians 9:8).

The work of caring can be so very demanding that those doing the work may very well wonder if they can find the strength needed. Paul insists that it is the Lord who will give to his people the strength to meet the needs of the moment.

The Apostle himself had a sparkling testimony to offer on this point. Three times he asked the Lord to remove a vexing physical ailment. While refusing to grant Paul's request, the Lord promised to give him grace to bear it, saying, 'My grace is sufficient for you, for my strength is made perfect in weakness' (2 Corinthians 12:9). God's grace is sufficient for his people in every situation and for every challenge.

God is glorified

Paul's words to the Corinthians yield a final consolation for carers. Christian carers can cause those who receive it to glorify God. Paul was, as we have noticed, appealing to the Corinthians to make a generous financial contribution to the saints in Jerusalem. He assures them that 'the administration of this service' would cause those beleaguered fellow-believers to abound in 'thanksgivings' to God and to 'glorify God' for the obedience of the Corinthians (2 Corinthians 9:12-13).

Ours is a time in which many profess to be disillusioned with Christianity. The church is left trying to figure out how to gain a hearing. We must, of course, be clear-headed and persuasive in presenting a well-reasoned case for the gospel. But we must also understand that we can win the argument without winning the heart. All God's people are called to win hearts by doing good (1 Peter 2:12), and Christian carers may rest assured that God has placed them in positions in which they can more easily and powerfully do so.

THINK ABOUT IT

On the night before his crucifixion, Jesus girded himself with a towel and washed the feet of his disciples (John 13:1-10). It was customary in Jesus' culture for the host of a dinner to provide a pitcher of water, a basin, a towel and a servant to wash the feet of arriving guests. The roads of those days were dusty, and one could not walk without getting his feet dirty. When Jesus and his disciples made the arrangements for their last supper together, they may have requested that the owner of the room leave them completely alone. The host had, therefore, provided the pitcher of water, the basin and the towel, but no servant.

In such a case, it fell to the lowest ranking person in the group to wash the feet of all the others. But none of the disciples were willing to admit that he was lower than the rest.

THINK ABOUT IT

It was against this backdrop that Jesus rose from his supper and assumed the role of the servant. He applied his washing of their feet in this way: 'You call me Teacher and Lord, and you say well, for so I am. If I then, your Lord and Teacher, have washed your feet, you also ought to wash one another's feet. For I have given you an example, that you should do as I have done to you' (John 13:13-15).

REMEMBER THIS

The Lord Jesus Christ is the supreme carer. Upon seeing the multitudes, Jesus was moved with compassion towards them because they were 'weary and scattered, like sheep having no shepherd' (Matthew 9:36).

We must all find ways to be Christian carers.

QUESTIONS FOR DISCUSSION

1. *Who are some well-known carers in the Bible? Read Luke 10:25-37; Acts 9:36; Philippians 2:25-30; 2 Timothy 1:16-18.*

2. *Read Romans 12:6-15. What qualities are essential for providing Christian care?*

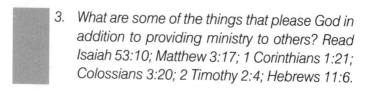

3. What are some of the things that please God in addition to providing ministry to others? Read Isaiah 53:10; Matthew 3:17; 1 Corinthians 1:21; Colossians 3:20; 2 Timothy 2:4; Hebrews 11:6.

CHAPTER NINETEEN

COMFORT FOR THE DYING

LOOK IT UP

BIBLE REFERENCE

Yea, though I walk through the valley of the shadow
of death
I will fear no evil;
For you are with me;
Your rod and your staff, they comfort me
(Psalm 23:4).

Suggested reading: 2 Corinthians 5:1-8

INTRODUCTION

A truth capsule

'If we knew what God knows about death, we would clap our hands.'[1]

(George MacDonald)

'Why should we then fear death, that is but a passage to Christ? It is but a grim sergeant that lets us into a glorious palace, that strikes off our bolts, that takes off our rags, that we may be clothed with better robes, that ends all our misery, and is the beginning of all our happiness. Why should we therefore be afraid of death, it is but a departure to a better condition.'[2]

(Richard Sibbes)

Some points to ponder

A comfortable view of death

We cannot read Psalm 23:4 without immediately gaining the impression that its author David was very comfortable with the prospect of death. There is no terror in the verse. There is, indeed, as Matthew Henry says, 'one word which sounds terrible'. That is the word 'death'.[3]

It is only natural for us to shrink from physical death, which is the separation of body and soul. Death is an intruder into God's creation. It came into this world as a result of mankind's sinful rebellion against God.

But, as Matthew Henry notes, the terror of the word 'death' quickly gives way to 'four words which lessen the terror'.[4]

'Shadow'

The first of these words is 'shadow'. A dark shadow may appear to be quite frightening but it has no real power to harm us. And death, unpleasant and forbidding as it may be, cannot finally do any real harm to the child of God. Henry T. Mahan writes: '...Christ has removed the substance of death and only a shadow remains. A shadow is there but cannot hurt or destroy.'[5]

'Valley'

The second of David's terror-lessening words is 'valley'. While admitting that the valley is 'deep indeed, and dark, and dirty', Matthew Henry calls it a fruitful place and concludes that death offers 'fruitful comforts to God's people'.[6]

⟨**THINK** ABOUT IT⟩

A twentieth-century Palestinian shepherd's explanation of the valley of the shadow of death explains why Henry would call it deep, dark and dirty. The shepherd writes:

There is an actual Valley of the Shadow of Death in Palestine, and every sheepherder from Spain to Dalmatia knows of it. It is south of the Jericho road leading from Jerusalem to the Dead Sea and is a narrow defile through a mountain range. Climactic and grazing conditions make it necessary for the sheep to be moved through this valley for seasonal feeding each year.

The valley is four and a half miles long. Its side walls are over 1,500 feet high in places and it is only ten or twelve feet wide at the bottom. Travel through the valley is dangerous, because its floor, badly eroded by cloudbursts, has gullies seven or eight feet deep. Actual footing of solid rock is so narrow in many places that sheep cannot turn round, and it is an unwritten law of shepherds that flocks must go up the valley in the morning hours and down towards the eventide, lest flocks meet in the defile. Mules have not been able to make the trip for centuries, but sheep and goat herders from earliest Old Testament days have maintained a passage for their stock.

About halfway through the valley the walk crosses from one side to the other at a place where the path is cut in two by an eight-foot gully. One section of the path is about eighteen inches higher than the other; the sheep must jump across it. The shepherd stands at this break and coaxes or forces the sheep to make the leap. If a sheep slips and lands in the gully, the shepherd's rod is brought into play. The old-style crook is encircled around a large sheep's neck or a small sheep's chest, and it is lifted to safety. If a more modern narrow crook is used, the sheep is caught about the hoofs and lifted up to walk.

Many wild dogs lurk in the shadows of the valley looking for prey. After a band of sheep has entered the defile, the leader may count upon such a dog. Unable to retreat, the leader 'baas' a warning. The shepherd, skilled in throwing his staff, hurls it at the dog and knocks the animal into the washed-out gully where it is easily killed. Thus the sheep have learned to fear no evil even in the Valley of the Shadow of Death, for their master is there to save them from harm.[7]

EXPLANATION

'Walk'

David describes his activity in the valley as walking, which is regarded as pleasant and restful.

'Through'

How thankful we should be for this word! The valley of death is not the stopping place for the children of God. It is a travelling place. Matthew Henry notes that the saints of God will not get lost in it but will come out safely.[8]

The basis of this comfortable view

How did David come to have such a tranquil view of death? Was this just wishful thinking on his part? Was it unwillingness to face reality? Or did David have a sure and solid basis for his tranquillity?

David himself gives us the answer. He writes:

I will fear no evil;
For you are with me;
Your rod and your staff, they comfort me.

(v. 4).

The Lord himself was the basis of David's peace about death. As David contemplates the end of his life he sees himself entering a dark valley.

Suddenly he is aware that someone else is there in the shadows. It is the Lord himself. As he gazes upon his Lord, David sees that he is carrying a rod and staff. The rod was a heavy club the shepherd used to kill predators, and the staff was a long pole with a crook in one end, used to round up the sheep and to guide them along.

The sight of those instruments made David realize that he had absolutely nothing to fear. His divine shepherd was there to kill the enemies of fear, doubt and guilt and to guide him safely through. The same Lord who had shepherded him through life (vv. 2-3) would shepherd him through death.

It is important to notice the change in emphasis as David reflects on his shepherd. In verses 2 and 3, David speaks about *his* shepherd (notice the fourfold use of 'he'). But when he comes to the valley of death, David drops the 'he' in favour of 'you' and 'your'. He was able to look upon the prospect of death with peace and tranquillity because he knew that it would mean meeting his glorious shepherd face to face.

If we would have the same peace about death as David we must have the same shepherd. As we consider this psalm we must always keep in mind that it is all predicated upon the opening line: 'The Lord is my shepherd.'

We cannot have what the shepherd produces without having the shepherd. We cannot have guidance and strength for this life (vv. 2-3), serenity about death (v. 4) and confidence about the life hereafter (v. 6), if we cannot heartily say with David, 'The LORD is my shepherd.'

It is not enough simply to say, 'The LORD is'. Merely acknowledging the existence of God does not approach what David said. Neither is it enough to say, 'The LORD is a shepherd.' Many are willing to acknowledge that there are people who find help and guidance in the Lord. On that basis they conclude that the Lord must indeed be a shepherd for some people.

If we want to enjoy the full measure of David's peace, we must have a full measure of faith. We must recognize that we desperately need a shepherd. We must recognize that only God can rightly shepherd us. And we must wholeheartedly turn to God, renouncing our reliance on ourselves and on any other shepherds.

THINK ABOUT IT

The Lord Jesus Christ made it wholly impossible for us to think about Psalm 23 without connecting it to him when he said, 'I am the good shepherd. The good shepherd gives his life for the sheep' (John 10:11).

REMEMBER THIS

A well-known American motel chain closes its commercials with these words: 'And we'll leave the light on for you.'

THINK ABOUT IT

That phrase takes me back to my early years in the ministry when various preaching assignments took me here and there. I often found myself driving many miles late at night. My mother always wanted to know my expected arrival time, and she would always say, 'We'll leave the light on for you.'

I remember looking forward to seeing that light. I would round the last curve, and see that brightly shining light. What a welcome, cheering sight it was! It spoke volumes to me. It told me my journey was over and I could now rest. It told me that my parents were concerned about me and were anxious for me to arrive.

The Bible constantly likens this life to a journey. The most difficult part of this journey comes at the end when we must go through the valley of death. What a dark, forbidding place that valley is! Most find their hearts trembling as they begin that deep descent.

What I am about to say sounds strange to modern ears, but that does not make it any less true: there is good news about death. We do not have to fear it. The Lord Jesus Christ has been there before us. He went down into that dark valley, but he did not stay there. He came out on the other side just as he promised. He decisively demonstrated his authority over death by rising from the grave.

He has also promised to use his authority over death on behalf of all those who know him as

Lord and Saviour. To each of them he says, 'Because I live, you will live also' (John 14:19).

Because of Christ, death will not have the final say over believers. When Jesus Christ returns, their bodies will arise from their graves and be transformed into the likeness of the Lord Jesus Christ himself. We do not have to worry about coming to our journey's end and getting safely through the valley of death. The Lord Jesus has been there, and he left the light on.

QUESTIONS FOR DISCUSSION

DISCUSS IT

1. Read 1 Thessalonians 4:13-18. What four specific promises does Paul include in these verses? Look for two promises in verse 16 and two in verse 17.

2. Read 1 Corinthians 15:50-58. What change does the believer have awaiting him? How long will this change take? When will this change occur? How should God's people live as they await this change?

3. Read 1 Corinthians 15:12-20. The Christian's hope is based on the resurrection of Christ. What is true if Christ did not arise? What is true if he did?

COMFORT FOR THE BEREAVED

BIBLE REFERENCE

'Then he took the child by the hand, and said to her, "Talitha, cumi," which is translated, "Little girl, I say to you, arise." Immediately the girl arose and walked, for she was twelve years of age. And they were overcome with great amazement'
(Mark 5:41-42).

Suggested reading: Luke 7:11-15

A truth capsule

The fifth chapter of Mark presents Jesus as the hope of the hopeless.[1] It first details how Jesus delivered a man who appeared to be hopelessly possessed by demons (vv. 1-20), and then how he healed a woman who appeared to be hopelessly sick (vv. 25-34). It then builds to a giant swelling crescendo with Jesus triumphing over an even more hopeless case, a case in which death had occurred. Jesus is truly the hope of the hopeless!

Some points to ponder

When Jairus set out to find Jesus, his daughter was desperately ill, but still alive. That was cause for at least a faint glimmer of hope. And Jesus had agreed to accompany Jairus to his home — a bright ray of hope! Now if they could just get there in time all would be well! But as Jairus observed the slow progress of Jesus through the enormous crowd, doubt began to set in. Then, to make matters worse, a woman interrupted Jesus by seeking healing. Jairus must have been heartened by this amazing demonstration of Jesus' healing power, but he also must have felt all hope melting down and oozing silently away.

Then suddenly it was all over! Jairus' worst fears were confirmed. Messengers appeared breathlessly before him and Jesus with the brutal words 'She's dead!' And hope gave one last flicker, and then it too died. R. C. H. Lenski captures the whole story in these crushing words: 'So Jairus had started for Jesus too late. Death outran him and won the race.'[2] All that was left for Jairus was to go home and tend to the wretched business of burying his daughter, and then spend the rest of his life 'kicking himself' for not seeking Jesus sooner.

Such is the story from Jairus' point of view. But what about Jesus? Was he prepared to join Jairus in declaring the situation hopeless and walking away in resignation? Not for a moment! In fact, when all others were throwing in the towel, Jesus was just rolling up his sleeves to go to work.

Silencing the voices of despair

The first thing he did was silence the voices of despair (vv. 35-40).

The voice of the messengers

The passage records two voices that spoke with despair. First there were the messengers who brought the heart-wrenching news. We do not know whether these people were relatives or friends, but they took it upon themselves to pronounce the situation hopeless. Notice the way they put it: 'Your daughter is dead. Why trouble the Teacher any further?' (v. 35). Instead of relating what had happened and then waiting to see if Jesus offered any hope, they assumed even Jesus could not do anything about death. Charles R. Eerdman says their words were 'enough to quench the hope of the most ardent believer'.[3]

These messengers were simply subscribing to the well-worn dogma of the day: 'Where there's life, there's hope.'

We've all said it. People have been saying it in one form or another ever since the author of Ecclesiastes penned these gloomy words: 'For him who is joined to all the living there is hope, for a living dog is better than a dead lion' (Ecclesiastes 9:4).

Before Jairus could be pulled down to the bottom of the pit of despair and covered with its mire, Jesus stepped in with these bold, decisive words: 'Do not be afraid; only believe' (v. 36). Precious words! Someone has counted 365 occurrences of 'Fear not' in the Bible — one for each day of the year!

Jairus had already shown faith by seeking out Jesus. He had disregarded what people would say about him, a ruler of the synagogue, casting himself at the feet of a man considered heretical by the religious authorities of the day. He had come to Jesus out of a deep awareness of his need and with great humility. He had shown willingness to do what Jesus said. In these ways he serves as an excellent model for all who would approach Christ. But now his faith was beginning to crumble, and he sorely needed these reassuring words from Jesus. Jesus was simply saying, 'You have believed up to this point, so do not stop now. Keep on believing.'

What the gloomy messengers did not understand is that there need be no limits placed on the power of Christ. He is just as able to raise the dead as he is to heal the sick. So the first thing Jesus did was to silence this voice of despair.

The voice of the mourners

But after Jesus and Jairus arrived at the house they encountered another voice of despair. This was the voice of the mourners.

THINK ABOUT IT

It was customary in the time of Jesus for families who lost a loved one to hire professional mourners. One rabbi is quoted as saying, 'Even the poorest in Israel should hire not less than two flutes and one wailing woman.'[4]

Because the dead had to be buried without delay in those days, these mourners arrived very soon after a death and began grieving with deafening wails and shrieks. This mourning might be extended for as much as a week although the dead person was usually buried on the same day as his death.

The only difference between this voice and the voice of the messengers is that this was the voice of emotion while the latter was the voice of reason. When despair sets in, it always operates in both realms. It argues against all the reasons we can muster for hope, and it overwhelms our spirits.

Jesus did not waste any more time dealing with this voice than he did with the first. He met it head on with these words: 'Why make this commotion and weep?' (v. 39). These words caused this voice of despair to speak again — this time in uproarious laughter (v. 40). The picture conveyed here is of people hooting and howling in derision. But Jesus, undaunted by the ridicule, took command of the situation and 'put them all outside' (v. 40).

We surely have no difficulty seeing how all this applies to us. Like Jairus, we are constantly being subjected to voices of despair beating on our minds and slamming against our emotions. Any time we see the need for God's power, we may be sure the voices of despair will start telling us why we cannot expect to see God work. Mention the need for revival and a chorus of voices will say the times are different, and people are too hardened for us to expect such an outpouring of God's Spirit. Mention wanting to see loved ones saved and the voices of despair will chime in unison: 'It's no use.'

Everyone who hears the voice of Christ calling him to salvation also hears the voices of despair saying, 'You are too great a sinner,' or 'You've put it off too long.'

Against all these voices sounds the voice of Christ saying, 'Only believe.' Listen to the voices of despair and you will have despair. Listen to the voice of Christ, and the despair will be replaced by peace, hope and joy.

Notice that Jesus did not stop with silencing the voices of despair. That in itself was not sufficient. He had to go on to show why these voices were wrong. He had to demonstrate his power.

Snatching the victory from death (vv. 41-43)

With the voices of despair not present to say why the dead girl could not be raised, a quiet dignity and an eager anticipation set in. It seems God never does his work with commotion and noise, but with quietness and calmness. How desperately urgent it is for us to learn this lesson! We are always in danger of making a great noise and calling it revival. Remember God spoke to Elijah not in wind, earthquake, or fire, but in 'a still small voice' (1 Kings 19:12). We shall not see a true work of God until we cease our religious noise and begin relying solely on the Spirit of God (see Isaiah 30:15; 32:17; Zechariah 4:6).

In that atmosphere of calm, Jesus stepped up to the little girl, took her by the hand and said, 'Talitha, cumi!' (v. 41).

Without a moment's hesitation the little girl arose and began to walk. She was completely and instantaneously restored! She was not even weak! Oh, the power of Christ — power to open the jaws of death and snatch away its prey!

Not only was this an astounding demonstration of the power of Christ, it served as notice to Satan and all his hosts that Christ would raid death of all those who believed in him. Outside the tomb of Lazarus, on a later occasion, Jesus gave the reason for his ability to defeat death. He said, 'I am the resurrection and the life. He who believes in me, though he may die, he shall live. And whoever lives and believes in me shall never die' (John 11:25-26).

Jesus has the power over death because he is God. If there could be any doubt after Jesus raised others from the dead, he himself came out of the grave. Paul says Christ's resurrection proved that Christ was the Son of God (Romans 1:4). And Christ, with this power to conquer death, has promised to raise to everlasting life all those who trust him as Lord and Saviour (John 14:19; 1 Corinthians 15:20-28).

Can you imagine the joy that flooded over Jairus and his family when they saw their loved one get up and walk? What a reunion that must have been! How does someone express his joy for such a thing? There must have been laughing and weeping, singing and dancing.

I do not know the details of their celebration, but I know all God's family will be gathered to their heavenly home some glorious day. What a day that will be! Loved ones will be reunited, tears will be wiped away, all the heavy burdens of life will be lifted, despair and death will be banished for ever, as the glorious, eternal day dawns.

So despair and death, do your utmost. You shall not win the victory over those who know Christ. The victory belongs to him and to his. To him be the praise for ever and ever!

THINK ABOUT IT

Selwyn Hughes mentions the following phrase from Samuel Coleridge: 'People with bedridden truths which lie asleep in the dormitory of their minds'. Hughes then makes this application: 'Many of us hold truths, but they are bedridden truths — they don't walk and dance and go in procession, with banners waving.'[5] The glorious truth of our Lord Jesus Christ having power over death should free us from bedridden truths and make us walk each day with banners waving.

REMEMBER THIS

REMEMBER THIS

John W. Drakeford offers the following suggestions for dealing with the bereaved:

1. Realize the gift of presence. Just calling and being there can be of value.
2. Do not talk too much yourself. Provide the awesome power of the listening ear.
3. Let them know it is alright for them to grieve. Even Jesus wept over the death of his friend Lazarus.
4. Be ready to minister to the griever for a long time. It sometimes takes as much as two years to work through a grief experience.
5. Tactfully remind them of he who said, 'I am the resurrection and the life. He who believes in me, though he may die, he shall live' (John 11:25), and invoke his blessing.[6]

QUESTIONS FOR DISCUSSION

1. Read Luke 7:11-17 and John 11:38-44. What do these accounts have in common?

2. Read Psalm 1. What does it say about the destiny of those who mock or scorn God's truth? How does this compare with that of the righteous?

3. Read Ephesians 2:1-10. What kind of death and resurrection does it discuss? To what does Paul attribute this kind of resurrection?

THE GUIDE

CHAPTER
TWENTY-ONE

COMFORT FOR THE STORM-TOSSED

LOOK IT UP

'Then the sea arose because a great wind was blowing. So when they had rowed about three or four miles, they saw Jesus walking on the sea and drawing near the boat; and they were afraid. But he said to them, "It is I; do not be afraid." Then they willingly received him into the boat, and immediately the boat was at the land where they were going' (John 6:18-21).

Suggested reading: Matthew 14:22-33

INTRODUCTION

A truth capsule

An hour or two was all that would have normally been necessary to cross the Sea of Galilee, but the disciples of Jesus would not have a normal crossing. They would not row very long before running into 'the mother of storms'.

The disciples' experience in this storm is full of meaning for all who know the Lord because we also have storms that suddenly come upon us and compel us to say with the poet:

When the storms of life are raging, stand by me.
When the storms of life are raging, stand by me.
When the world is tossing me like a ship upon the sea,
Thou who rulest wind and water, stand by me.[1]

THINK ABOUT IT

This miracle was performed hard on the heels of the feeding of the five thousand. It was also performed in the presence of Jesus' disciples alone. These two facts seem to demand one conclusion: the feeding of the five thousand did something to the disciples that made this particular sign necessary. What did this miracle do to the disciples? John supplies us with the answer when he says it caused the multitude to want to seize Jesus and make him king (v. 15).

What did that have to do with the disciples? Jesus knew they were easy prey for the emotion of that moment. They shared the common belief of the crowd that the Messiah's kingdom would be a material, political kingdom. Nothing would have pleased them more than for Jesus to declare himself king, lead a triumphant multitude to Jerusalem, throw off Roman rule, and bring peace and prosperity to Israel.

We have a very difficult time understanding how deeply etched this view was in the Jewish mind. So engrained was it that the disciples themselves were still clinging to it after Jesus' death and resurrection. It was only after he ascended into heaven that they finally seemed to understand that his kingdom is spiritual in nature (Acts 1:6-11).

EXPLANATION

Some points to ponder

When the crowd began clamouring for Jesus to be their king, he rose to the challenge by doing three things. First, he ordered his disciples to get into their boat and row to the other side of the lake. John simply says, 'His disciples went down to the sea' (v. 16). Matthew and Mark say they did so because Jesus 'made' them get into the boat and start crossing the sea. In other words, Jesus took charge of the situation and prevented his disciples from getting carried away with the crowd's mistaken notion of kingship.

Secondly, he sent the multitude away. How does one just dismiss a multitude that is caught in a fever pitch of excitement? It was no problem for Jesus. His majestic, authoritative word was more than sufficient for the task.

Finally, Jesus himself retired to seek his Father's face in prayer. Here he was confronted again with the temptation Satan used in the wilderness immediately after his baptism, that is, the temptation to bypass the cross and simply seize the crown (Matthew 4:8-9).

If anything, the temptation here was even stronger than on the previous occasion. The first time, only one solitary voice whispered enchantingly; but here there were five thousand voices which thundered it passionately.

THINK ABOUT IT

The feeding of the five thousand and Jesus' stilling of the storm are two of seven 'signs' reported by John's Gospel. The other signs are as follows:

- Changing water into wine — 2:1-11
- Healing the nobleman's son — 4:46-54
- Healing the man at the pool of Bethesda — 5:1-9
- Healing the blind man — 9:1-7
- Raising Lazarus from the dead — 11:38-44

But let us get back to the disciples. They are now in the boat and rowing their way to the other side of the Sea of Galilee. As already stated, normally it would only have taken them an hour or two to complete the crossing, but on this occasion, soon after they had begun their journey, they suddenly ran into a tremendous storm.

All who know the Lord can easily identify with the disciples here, when we too face unexpected trials. How do we find the strength to deal with them? The disciples' experience yields two major truths that are able to help all Christians who are in the grip of a storm.

Jesus sent them into the storm

First, Jesus sent them into the storm. John goes out of his way in this Gospel to make clear that Jesus was no ordinary man and that he had, therefore, extraordinary knowledge. One of the things John says is that Jesus knew all men (2:24). This was proven later when Jesus told the Samaritan woman all about her past (4:17-18).

If Jesus had this kind of extraordinary knowledge, there was no need for him to listen to Galilee's local weather forecast on GLEE - 103. The truth is, Jesus knew the storm was coming because he ordered it to come. After the storm was over, we do not find him saying, 'If I had known a storm was brewing I would not have sent you out.'

Why would Jesus do this to his disciples? Why would he order a storm and then make them sail into it? As we have noted, they had become very excited at the idea of Jesus being king. So Jesus wanted to teach them in a powerful and unforgettable way what his kingship was like. The crowd had it all wrong. His kingdom was not designed simply to bring his followers ease and comfort. It was not just to free them from problems and increase their standard of living. By sending the disciples into the storm Jesus was showing them that he had called them away from a life of ease to a life of hardship and difficulty.

Do we need this lesson today? The indications are that we do. Multitudes have accepted a Christianity that requires nothing of them. They follow God for one reason and one reason alone: for what they can get out of it. If you talk to them about sacrifice, and commitment, and trials, they will quickly tell you that you do not understand Christianity. As far as these people are concerned, the biblical teachings that we have been called to suffer have no application to us at all (Philippians 1:29; 2 Timothy 3:12; 1 Peter 4:12).

What happens when God's people get caught up and carried away by the notion that God exists just to bring us ease and happiness? The Lord may just send a storm our way as he did with his twelve disciples. He still draws his people away from the perversity of the world and purifies their faith by sending storms and trials.

Knowing the Lord has a purpose for us in the storms of life, that they are designed to wean us away from a godless world, makes them easier to bear.

Jesus came to them in the storm

There is something else that makes storms easier to bear. As we note the disciples' experience with the storm, we see Jesus came to them in the midst of the storm. Notice three things about Jesus coming to them.

1. Jesus' delay

First, he came after a long delay. The storm unleashed its fury upon the disciples shortly after they set sail. For a period of several hours they had struggled and toiled. Jesus, of course, knew they were in the storm. Remember, he is the one who ordered it, and Mark's

EXPLANATION

Gospel suggests he actually saw them from the mountain where he had been praying (Mark 6:48). Are you ready for this? Even though the storm was severe and even though they were fearful and exhausted, Jesus just let them toil.

Why this delay? Why didn't Jesus immediately come to their aid? Don't we also expect the Lord to come immediately to our aid when we find ourselves facing a crisis or difficulty? It is very hard for us to understand this, but the Lord's delays are also for our good. It is only as the trial takes its course and our strength is spent that we see how desperately we need him.

The disciples had undoubtedly reached that point of desperation and thought Jesus had completely forsaken them. Then he came. Here's the second truth we must note — when he came they were afraid of him!

2. The disciples' fear

Can you imagine such a thing? They knew from Jesus' healing of the nobleman's son that he could work miracles from afar (John 4:46-54). Perhaps they were expecting him to do the same in this situation. The one thing they did not seem to expect was Jesus coming towards them walking on the water. They should not have been surprised. They had seen great miracles that very day, but their faith was so small and their hearts were so hard that they were caught completely off guard.

As a matter of fact, most of us are not much better than the disciples. When a trial comes we, like them, spend a great deal of time wondering why it has happened and where the Lord is. And when the Lord does come to us to speak words of comfort and peace we are slow to believe and respond.

Sometimes we allow ourselves to become so bitter about the storm that we actually shut ourselves off from the comfort available to us in the Word of God and in the house of God.

That brings us to the final truth, that is, when Jesus came it was with mighty power.

3. Jesus' power

In actual fact, there were really two storms raging that night. One was the storm that tossed the ship and caused the disciples to strain their bodies. The other was the one that tossed their hearts and strained their faith.

Consider how these men must have felt when Jesus commanded them to get into the boat and cross the sea. That was the last thing they wanted to do. All the excitement was there with Jesus and the multitude. The moment they had been living for had finally arrived. Jesus was being popularly acclaimed as king!

They had to carry heavy hearts with them as they climbed into that boat. All their hopes and fondest

EXPLANATION

dreams had been dashed and questions must have begun to arise. Was Jesus really the Messiah? How could he do these miracles if he wasn't? But if he was the Messiah why was he so reluctant to claim his rightful throne? If the people were on his side, what was there to be gained by waiting?

When Jesus finally came to them and stilled the storm raging around their boat he also stilled the storm in their hearts. There could be no doubt about whether he was the Messiah. Anyone who has the wind and waves at his beck and call has to be king!

By calming the storm Jesus was saying in effect, 'Just because I have refused to be king on the basis of bread does not mean I'm not king. I will be king on my own terms, not on the basis of what is popular.'

The message got through to the disciples. John says they received him willingly into the boat. Matthew says they fell down and worshipped him (Matthew 14:33).

REMEMBER THIS

Has the message come through to you? Jesus Christ is King of kings and Lord of lords! The test of whether it has come through is worshipping him. Anyone who really believes Jesus is King cannot help but worship. Anyone who refuses to worship only shows he does not really believe Jesus is King.

QUESTIONS FOR DISCUSSION

1. Read John 11:1-15 for another example of Jesus delaying before responding to a crisis. What reason did he give for this delay?

2. Read Matthew 28:18-20. How much power does Jesus claim to have? What did Jesus call his disciples to do in the light of his power?

3. Read Acts 27. How did Paul conduct himself in the terrible storm described in this chapter? How does his response compare to that of the disciples in John 6?

THE GUIDE

NOTES

NOTES

Chapter 1
1. D. James Kennedy, *Why I Believe*, Word Books, p.48.

Chapter 2
1. From the hymn 'When the morning comes' by Charles A. Tindley (1851-1933).
2. From the hymn 'The sands of time are sinking' by Anne Ross Cousin (1824-1906).

Chapter 3
1. Adrian Rogers, *Mastering Your Emotions*, Broadman Press, p.155.
2. Cited by R. Kent Hughes, *Preaching the Word: James*, Crossway Books, p.22.
3. Selwyn Hughes, *Every Day Light: Treasure for the Heart*, Broadman & Holman Publishers, p.79.

Chapter 4
1. Cited by Hughes, *Every Day Light*, p.31.

Chapter 5
1. From the hymn 'He giveth more grace' by Annie Johnson Flint (1866-1932).

Chapter 6
1. D. James Kennedy, *Truths that Transform*, Fleming H. Revell Company, pp.99-100.
2. Cliff Barrows, ed., *Crusader Hymns and Hymn Stories*, The Billy Graham Evangelistic Association, p.51.

3. Rogers, *Mastering Your Emotions*, p.137.

Chapter 7
1. O. S. Hawkins, *Moral Earthquakes and Secret Faults*, Broadman & Holman Publishers, p.19.

Chapter 9
1. Eldon Woodcock: *Bible Study Commentary: Proverbs*, Zondervan Publishing House, pp.40-2.

Chapter 10
1. D. Martyn Lloyd-Jones, *Preaching and Preachers*, Zondervan Publishing House, p.175.
2. From the hymn 'Rescue the perishing' by Fanny J. Crosby (1820-1915).
3. J. D. Douglas, ed., *The New International Dictionary of the Christian Church*, Zondervan Publishing House, p.272.

Chapter 11
1. *Expositions of Holy Scripture: Ezekiel, Daniel and the Minor Prophets*, Baker Book House, p.248.

Chapter 12
1. Earl D. Radmacher, ed., *Can We Trust the Bible?*, Tyndale House Publishers, Inc., p.9.
2. Josh McDowell, *The New Evidence that Demands a Verdict*, Thomas Nelson Publishers, p.7.
3. As above, pp.168-92.

Chapter 13
1. Trent C. Butler, ed., *Holman Bible Dictionary*, Holman Bible Publishers, p.378.
2. As above, p.518.

Chapter 14
1. E. M. Blaiklock, *Bible Study Commentary: The Pastoral Epistles*, Zondervan Publishing House, p.123.
2. Geoffrey B. Wilson, *The Pastoral Epistles*, The Banner of Truth Trust, p.166.
3. As above, p.167.
4. Warren Wiersbe, *Lonely People*, Back to the Bible Publications, p.7.

Chapter 15
1. James Montgomery Boice, *Psalms*, Baker Book House, vol. ii, p.520.

Chapter 16
1. J. A. Thompson, 'Sackcloth', *New Bible Dictionary*, J. D. Douglas, ed., Wm B. Eerdmans Publishing Co., p.1112.
2. Albert Barnes, *Notes on the Old Testament: Isaiah*, Baker Book House, vol.i, p.485.
3. From the hymn 'Face to face with Christ' by Carrie E. Breck (1855-1934).

Chapter 17
1. From the hymn 'Amazing grace' by John Newton (1725-1807).
2. *Crusader Hymns and Hymn Stories*, Cliff Barrows ed., The Billy Graham Evangelistic Association, p.7.

Chapter 18
1. Geoffrey B. Wilson, *Hebrews*, The Banner of Truth Trust, p.80.
2. Cited by Wilson, *Hebrews*, p.80.

Chapter 19
1. Cited by J. I. Packer, *I Want to be a Christian*, Tyndale House Publishers, Inc., p.162.
2. Richard Sibbes, *Works of Richard Sibbes*, The Banner of Truth Trust, vol.i, p.340.
3. Matthew Henry, *Matthew Henry's Commentary*, Fleming H. Revell Company, vol. iii, p.318.
4. As above.
5. Henry T. Mahan, *With New Testament Eyes*, Evangelical Press, vol.ii, pp.18-9.
6. Henry, *Commentary*, p.318.
7. Joel R. Beeke, *Jehovah Shepherding His Flock*, Reformation Heritage Books, pp.214-5.
8. Henry, *Commentary*, p.318.

Chapter 20
1. William Hendriksen, *New Testament Commentary: Mark*, Baker Book House, p.216.
2. R. C. H. Lenski, *The Interpretation of St. Mark's Gospel*, Augsburg Publishing House, p.217.
3. Charles R. Eerdman, *The Gospel of Mark*, The Westminster Press, p.89.
4. James A. Brooks, *The New American Commentary: Mark*, Broadman Press, p. 94.
5. Hughes, *Every Day Light*, p.100.
6. *Holman Bible Dictionary*, p. 585.

Chapter 21
1. From the hymn 'Stand by me' by Charles A. Tindley (1851-1933).

A wide range of excellent books on spiritual subjects is available from Evangelical Press. Please write to us for your free catalogue or contact us by e-mail.

Evangelical Press
Faverdale North Industrial Estate, Darlington,
DL3 0PH, England

Evangelical Press USA
P. O. Box 825, Webster, New York 14580, USA

e-mail: sales@evangelicalpress.org

web: www.evangelicalpress.org